The Invisible Man

CBSE Class XII

English-Hindi

ARIHANT PRAKASHAN, MEERUT

ARIHANT PRAKASHAN, MEERUT

Administrative & Production Offices

Corporate Office 4577/15, Agarwal Road, Darya Ganj, New Delhi -110002
Tele: 011- 47630600, 23280316; Fax: 011- 23280316

Head Office Kalindi, TP Nagar, Meerut (UP) - 250002
Tele: 0121-2401479; Fax: 0121-2401648

Sales & Support Offices

Agra, Ahmedabad, Bengaluru, Bhubaneswar, Chennai, Delhi(I&II), Guwahati, Haldwani, Hyderabad, Jaipur, Kolkata, Kota, Lucknow, Nagpur, Meerut, Patna & Pune

ISBN 978-93-5176-530-1

Typeset by Arihant DTP Unit at Meerut

For further information about the products from Arihant, log on to www.arihantbooks.com or email to info@arihantbooks.com

Preface

The CBSE, in order to develop the habit of long-text reading in students, has introduced this novel in curriculum of class XII English Core. This book is prescribed keeping in view the lightness of the text and simplicity of the plot of the novel so that students will enjoy reading it.

The Invisible Man is a science fiction novella by HG Wells published in 1897. Originally serialised in Pearsons Weekly in 1897, it was published as a novel, the same year. Initially the novel contained 28 chapters, but Wells added the epilogue to the American edition and it wasnt in the original magazine version. The Invisible Man of the title is Griffin, a scientist who has devoted himself to research into optics and invents a way to change a bodys refractive index to that of air so that it absorbs and reflects no light and thus becomes invisible.

This series has been specially prepared with the purpose to make the reading of novels easy and less time consuming. The novel has been covered in English & Hindi Language both because reading in English is takes more time than in Hindi. For this reason, we have tried to make the reading easy by giving the material in both Hindi & English Language, so that the students can understand the content of the novels in a comfortable way and then write the perfect answers.

We have tried to help out the students in all aspects to learn this novel in such a way that they will become competent enough to answer the questions that will be asked in exams. We hope the student will relish this book.

Novel Outline

About the Novel

The Invisible Man is a science fiction **novella** by H. G. Wells published in 1897. Originally serialised in Pearsons Weekly in 1897, it was published as a novel the same year. The Invisible Man of the title is Griffin, a scientist who has devoted himself to research into optics and invents a way to change a bodys refractive index to that of air so that it absorbs and reflects no light and thus becomes invisible. He successfully carries out this procedure on himself, but fails in his attempt to reverse the procedure.

While its predecessors, The Time Machine and The Island of Doctor Moreau, were written using first person narrators, Wells adopts a third Plot summary person objective point of view in **The Invisible Man.**

Plot Summary

A mysterious stranger, Griffin, arrives at the local inn of the English village of Iping, West Sussex, during a snowstorm. The stranger wears a long-sleeved, thick coat and gloves, his face hidden entirely by bandages except for a fake pink nose and a wide-brimmed hat. He is excessively reclusive, irascible and unfriendly. He demands to be left alone and spends most of his time in his rooms working with a set of chemicals and laboratory apparatus, only venturing out at night. While staying at the inn, hundreds of strange glass bottles arrive that Griffin calls his luggage. Many local townspeople believe this to be very strange. He becomes the talk of the village (one of the novels most charming aspects is its portrayal of small town life in **Southern England**, which the author knew from first hand experience).

Meanwhile, a mysterious burglary occurs in the village. Griffin has run out of money and is trying to find a way to pay for his lodging. When his landlady demands, he pay his bill she and accuses him to burglary, he reveals part of his invisibility to her in a fit of pique. An attempt to apprehend the stranger is frustrated when he undresses to take advantage of his invisibility, fights off his would be captors and flees to the downs.

There Griffin coerces a tramp, **Thomas Marvel**, into becoming his assistant. With Marvel, he returns to the village to recover three notebooks that contain records of his experiments. When Marvel attempts to betray the Invisible Man and run away with his most priced possessions, Griffin chases him to the seaside town of Port Burdock, threatening to kill him. Marvel escapes to a local inn and is saved by the people at the inn, but Griffin escapes. Marvel later goes to the police and tells them of this invisible Man, then requests to be locked up in a high security jail.

Griffins furious attempts to avenge his betrayal leads to his being shot. He takes shelter in a nearby house that turns out to belong to Dr Kemp a former acquaintance from medical school. To Kemp, he reveals his true identity, the Invisible Man is Griffin, a former medical student who left medicine to devote himself to optics. Griffin recounts how he invented procedure capable of rendering bodies invisible and on impulse, performed the procedure on himself.

Griffin tells Kemp of the story of how he became invisible. He explains how he tried the invisibility on a cat, then himself. Griffin burns down the boarding house he is staying in along with all his equipment he used to turn invisible to cover his tracks, but soon realises he is ill-equipped to survive in the open. He attempts to steal food and clothes from a large department store and eventually steals some clothing from a theatrical supply shop and heads to Iping to attempt to reverse the invisibility. But now he imagines that he can make Kemp his secret confederate, describing his plan to begin a "Reign of Terror" by using his invisibility to terrorise the nation.

Kemp has already denounced Griffin to the local authorities and is watching for help to arrive as he listens to this wild proposal. When the authorities arrive at Kemps house, Griffin fights his way out and the next day leaves a note announcing that Kemp himself will be the first man to be killed in the "Reign of Terror". Kemp, a cool-headed character, tries to organise a plan to use himself as bait to trap the Invisible Man, but a note he sends is stolen from his servant by Griffin.

Griffin shoots and injures a local policeman who comes to Kemps aid, then breaks into Kemps house. Kemp bolts for the town, where the local citizes comes to his aid. Griffin is seized, assaulted and killed by a mob. The Invisible Man naked, battered body gradually becomes visible as he dies. A local policeman shouts to cover his face with a sheet, then the book concludes.

In the epilogue, it is revealed that Marvel has secretly kept Griffin notes. He hopes of deciphering their mystery some day and gain goldly powers.

Novel के बारे में...

"The Invisible Man", H.G. Wells के द्वारा रचित एक विज्ञानी **छोटी कहानी** है जो 1897 में छपी थी। शुरूआत में यह पीयरसंस नामक साप्ताहिकी में क्रमिक रूप से छपा करती थी पर उसी साल यह एक उपन्यास के रूप में भी छपी थी। शीर्षक का अदृश्य आदमी ग्रिफिन नामक एक वैज्ञानिक है जिसने अपनी सारी प्रतिभा उस शोध में लगा दी जिसका संबंध प्रकाश-भौतिकी से था। उसने गहन शोध करके शरीर का अपवर्तनांक इतना कम करने का एक तरीका खोज निकाला था कि यह हवा के अपवर्तनांक के बराबर हो गया था और इसके फलस्वरूप शरीर प्रकाश की किरणों को अवशोषित कर लेता था तथा प्रकाश की कोई किरण परावर्तित नहीं होती थी। इसका नतीजा यह हुआ कि शरीर अदृश्य हो गया था। उसने अपने शरीर के ऊपर यह प्रयोग सफलतापूर्वक कर लिया पर इसके परिणाम को पलटने में नाकाम रहा।

वेल्स के पिछले दो उपन्यास "The time machine" तथा "The Island of doctor moreau" प्रथम पुरुष में लिखे गए थे पर **Invisible Man** में इन्होंने अन्य पुरुष को ध्यान में लेते हुए कथानक तैयार किया।

Plot Summary

एक रहस्यमयी अजनबी, ग्रिफिन, ब्रिटेन के वेस्ट ससेक्स के आइपिंग गाँव में बर्फबारी के समय एक धर्मशाला में आता है। ग्रिफिन ने पूरी बाँहों वाला एक मोटा सा कोट तथा दस्ताने पहन रखे थे। उसके पूरे चेहरे पर पट्टी बँधी थी तथा उसकी नाक की जगह एक पीले रंग की नकली नाक लगा हुई थी। ग्रिफिन ने एक चौड़ी पट्टी वाली टोपी भी पहन रखी थी। वह अत्यधिक एकाकी, चिड़चिड़ा तथा अमित्रवत था। दिन में अधिकांश समय वह अकेला अपने कमरे में बंद रहता तथा रसायनों के साथ कार्य करता रहता था। केवल रात को वह बाहर निकलता था। धर्मशाला में निवास के दौरान ग्रिफिन का सामान आया था जो कि सैकड़ों की संख्या में अजीब तरह के काँच की बोतलें थीं। कई शहरी लोगों को लगता था कि यह सब कुछ अजीब है। ग्रिफिन पूरे गाँव में चर्चा का विषय बन गया था। (इस उपन्यास की सबसे खास बात थी लेखक द्वारा **दक्षिणी इंग्लैंड** के छोटे शहर की जीवनचर्या का विवरण जो कि लेखक को अच्छी तरह से ज्ञात था।)

इस बीच गाँव में एक रहस्यमय चोरी की घटना हुई। ग्रिफिन के सारे पैसे खत्म हो चुके थे और उसे अपने मकान-मालिक को किराये के पैसे देने थे। जब उसके मकान-मालिक ने उससे पैसे माँगे तो उसने उसे पैसे दे दिए पर गाँव में हुई चोरी का इल्जाम उस पर लगा दिया गया। गुस्से में आकर उसने उसको आधी अदृश्यता का अहसास करा दिया। बाद में उसने अपने कपड़े उतारे तथा अपनी अदृश्यता का लाभ लेकर अपने पकड़ने वालों को धक्का दिया तथा वहाँ से भाग निकला।

रास्ते में ग्रिफिन को एक घुमक्कड़ मिला जिसका नाम था **थॉमस मार्वेल**, जिसे उसने अपना सहायक बना लिया था। मार्वेल के साथ वह आइपिंग वापस आया तथा अपनी तीन नोटबुक, जिसमें उसके प्रयोग दर्ज थे, को लेने के लिए आया। जब मार्वेल ने ग्रिफिन को धोखा देने तथा उसकी तीन बहुमूल्य चीजों को गायब करने की सोची तो पोर्ट बॅर्डाक में उसने उसे जान से मारने की धमकी दी। मार्वेल ने जान बचाने के लिए पास की एक धर्मशाला में छिपने का फैसला किया। धर्मशाला के लोगों ने मार्वेल को बचा लिया पर ग्रिफिन वहाँ से भाग गया। इसके बाद मार्वेल पुलिस स्टेशन गया तथा पुलिस को सारी घटना की जानकारी दी। मार्वेल ने पुलिस से निवेदन किया कि उसे एक उच्च सुरक्षा वाले कक्ष में बंद कर दिया जाए।

ग्रिफिन ने धोखे का बदला लेने का प्रण नहीं छोड़ा और वह पास के एक घर में जाकर छिप गया। यह घर ग्रिफिन के एक साथी डॉ. कैंप का था जिसे वह मेडिकल स्कूल के समय से जानता था। कैंप के सामने ग्रिफिन ने अपनी वास्तविक पहचान जाहिर कर दी और उसे बताया कि एक मेडिकल का छात्र प्रकाश-भौतिकी को समर्पित हो गया था। उसने बताया कि उसके प्रयोग की वजह से वह अदृश्य हो गया है और अपने प्रयोग के सारे तरीके का वर्णन उसे बताया।

ग्रिफिन ने कैंप को अपनी अदृश्यता से जुड़ी सारी घटना बताई। उसने बताया कि उसने पहले एक बिल्ली को अदृश्य किया बाद में खुद को। ग्रिफिन ने जिस घर में यह सारे प्रयोग किए थे उस पूरे घर को आग लगा दी ताकि वह अपने पीछे कोई सबूत न छोड़े। पर जब वह सर्दी में बाहर निकला तो उसे पता चला कि वह इतनी सर्दी में रह नहीं पाएगा। उसने एक बड़े स्टोर से खाना व कपड़े चुराए तथा एक नाटक कंपनी से कुछ नकली सामान भी चुराए। इसके बाद अपने प्रयोग को आगे बढ़ाने के लिए वह आइपिंग की तरफ चला गया। ग्रिफिन ने सोचा कि वह कैंप को अपना राजदार बनाएगा। ग्रिफिन ने कैंप को अपने आतंक का राज कायम करने की बात बताई और कहा कि वह अपनी अदृश्यता को आतंक पैदा करने में इस्तेमाल करेगा।

जब कैंप उसके प्रस्ताव को ध्यान से सुन रहा था तो वह वास्तव में प्रशासन से मदद केइंतजार में बैठा था। उसने प्रशासन को ग्रिफिन और उसके इरादों के बारे में पहले ही बता दिया था। जैसे ही प्रशासन के लोग कैंप के घर पर आए तभी ग्रिफिन ने अपनी अदृश्यता का लाभ उठा कर अपने आप को वहाँ से सुरक्षित निकाल लिया। बाहर आने के बाद ग्रिफिन ने कैंप के नाम एक नोट लिखा और उसमें यह घोषणा की कि आतंक के राज में मरने वाला पहला व्यक्ति कैंप ही होगा। कैंप ने शांतचित्त होकर एक योजना बनाई कि वह अपने आप को ग्रिफिन को पकड़ने में एक चारे के तौर पर काम करेगा। पर कैंप का एक नोट ग्रिफिन द्वारा उसके नौकर से छीन लिया गया।

ग्रिफिन ने गोली चलाकर एक पुलिसवाले को घायल कर दिया जो कैंप की मदद के लिए आया था। इसके बाद वह कैंप के घर में घुस गया। कैंप अपने घर से शहर की तरफ भागा और सभी लोगों से मदद माँगने लगा। आसपास के लोगों ने ग्रिफिन को पकड़ लिया, उसे घेर कर मार दिया। जैसे ही ग्रिफिन की मौत हुई उसका अदृश्य शरीर दुबारा से दिखने लगा। एक पुलिसवाले ने उसे एक सफेद चादर से ढकने को कहा।

कहानी के अंत में यह बात जाहिर हो जाती है कि मार्वेल ने वह तीन किताबें अपने पास रखी हैं और उनकी कूट भाषा को समझने की कोशिश करता है। उसे उम्मीद थी कि वह भी एक दिन उसे समझ लेगा और खुद में जादुई शक्ति का मालिक बन जाएगा।

Know the **Characters...**

The Invisible Man

The Invisible Man is given many names in the novel. Though he is the protagonist of the story, all his deeds are more like that of an antagonist. He is an eccentric scientist. He loses his temper over petty things and starts hurting others. He has lost all sense of conscience.

Mrs Hall

Mrs Hall, is the owner of the **Coach and Horses** inn in Iping. She appears to be an opportunist. She gives the stranger a room in her inn. She accommodates with Griffins rudeness and awkward behaviour only because she was being paid. She is a dominating wife and doesn't shy away from giving her husband a lecture. When she had enough of the stranger's rudeness, she decided to set him straight and stopped serving him.

Mr Hall

Mr Hall is the husband of Mrs Hall and drove the Iping conveyance. He is a drunkard and his wife manages the inn on her own. He believes when Teddy Henfrey told him about Griffin. He wanted to know the details about his guest and tried to inspect his room when he found it empty. However, He gets taken to task by her many times. George is also kind like his wife. When the dog attacked Griffin, he rushed to his room to see if he needed any kind of help..

Mr Jaffers

Mr Jaffers is the constable of the Iping village who comes with a warrant to arrest the Invisible Man. He takes his work rather seriously. He comments that head or no head, he got to arrest him and that is what he will do. Apparently, he was hurt for he had failed to complete his duties and later we find him sunk in gloom.

Dr Kemp

Like Griffin, Dr Kemp was also a scientist. He lives in **Burdock**. He was a tall and slender young man with flaxen hair and a moustache almost white. He is very calm and sensible man who thought of the greater good. He goes to the extent of making himself a bait to catch Griffin.

Colonel Adye

Colonel Adye is the Chief of Police in Burdock. He is a brave man. He is a moral being but a bit foolish too. He comes to aid Dr Kemp to catch the Invisible Man. He tried his best but couldn't catch the Invisible Man. He is one of the victims in the story.

Mr Heelas

Mr Heelas was the next door neighbor to Dr Kemp. He was one of the sturdy minority who refused to believe in the story of the Invisible Man. He has a 'seeing then believing' attitude. However, he comes about as a coward who would not open his door to help his neighbour in distress.

Novel में उपस्थित प्रमुख व्यक्ति

अदृश्य आदमी

अदृश्य आदमी को उपन्यास में कई नाम दिए गए हैं। हालाँकि वह कहानी का मुख्य पात्र है पर उसका काम नकारात्मक रहा है। वह एक सनकी वैज्ञानिक है। छोटी-छोटी बातों पर वह अपना आपा खो देता है और दूसरों को चोट पहुँचाना शुरू कर देता है। वह अपने आप में नहीं होता और नैतिक पतन की ओर चला जाता है।

मिसेज हॉल

मिसेज हॉल आइपिंग के धर्मशाला **कोच एंड हॉर्सेज** की मालकिन हैं। वह एक अवसरवादी महिला है। ग्रिफिन को उसने अपने धर्मशाला में एक कमरा दिया था। ग्रिफिन के बुरे व्यवहार और बदतमीजियों को भी वह सिर्फ इसलिए झेल जाती है क्योंकि उसे उसके बदले में पैसे मिल रहे होते हैं। वह अपने पति को भी ताने मारने से बाज नहीं आती है और हमेशा उसकी खिंचाई करती रहती है। अदृश्य आदमी के व्यवहार से जब वह दु:खी हो गई तो उसने उसे खाना देना बंद कर दिया था।

मि हॉल

मि हॉल मिसेज हॉल के पति हैं और धर्मशाला परविहन का ध्यान रखते हैं। वह शराबी है और मिसेज हॉल धर्मशाला को खुद सँभाल रही होती है। टेडी हेनफ्रे के कहने पर उसने ग्रिफिन की विचित्रता का अनुमान पूरे भरोसे के साथ कर लिया था। मि हॉल अजनबी के बारे में जानना चाहता था और जब उसने उसका कमरा खाली देखा तो उसकी जाँच भी की थी। मि हॉल को कई बार अपनी पत्नी के गुस्से का सामना भी करना पड़ा था। मि हॉल दयालु स्वभाव का भी था। जब एक कुत्ते ने ग्रिफिन पर हमला कर दिया था तो वह ग्रिफिन के कमरे में उसे मदद के लिए पूछने गया था।

मि जैफर्स

मि जैफर्स आइपिंग गाँव में सिपाही था और गिरफ्तारी के वारंट के साथ वह ग्रिफिन को पकड़ने आए थे। वे कर्त्तव्यनिष्ठ थे। उसने कहा था सिर हो या न हो वह उसे गिरफ्तार करके रहेंगे। अफसोस कि वे ग्रिफिन को गिरफ्तार नहीं कर पाए और अपनी कर्त्तव्यनिष्ठता साबित नहीं कर पाए। इससे उन्हें घोर निराशा हुई थी।

डॉ केंप

ग्रिफिन की तरह ही डॉ केंप भी एक वैज्ञानिक थे। वे **बॅर्डाक** में रहते थे। वह लंबे कद के छरहरे इंसान थे। उनके बाल भूरे थे और सफेद मूँछें थी। वे सुलझे हुए इंसान थे और समाज के हित की बात करते थे। ग्रिफिन को पकड़वाने के लिए वे अपनी खुद की जान की बाजी लगाने को तैयार थे।

कर्नल एडी

कर्नल एडी बॅर्डाक की पुलिस के प्रमुख थे। वह एक बहादुर इंसान थे। वे नैतिक रूप से सक्षम तथा सहभागिता पूर्ण इंसान थे। वह कभी-कभी बेवकूफी भरी हरकत भी कर देते थे। वे ग्रिफिन को पकड़ने व डॉ केंप की मदद करने आए थे। उन्होनें अपना सबसे उत्तम प्रयास किया पर उसे पकड़ नहीं पाए। कहानी में ग्रिफिन के शिकारों में से वह भी एक थे।

मि हीलास

मि हीलास डॉ केंप के पड़ोसी थे। वे उन चुनिंदा लोगों में से एक थे जो अदृश्य आदमी की कहानी में यकीन नहीं करते थे। वह देखकर यकीन करने वाले लोगों में से थे। जब डॉ. केंप अपनी जान बचाने के लिए भाग रहे थे तब हीलास ने उनको अपने घर में जगह देने से मना कर दिया था।

The Invisibile Man

The Strange Man's Arrival

The Stranger at Iping

The story begins with a stranger arriving at the Bramblehurst railway station. It is February and probably the snowstorm is at its fury. He is wrapped from head to toe with only his shiny pink nose in the view. He is also wearing blue spectacles. He enters the inn named 'Coach and Horses' and asks for a room.

An Unusual Time for the Visit

It is nail biting cold in Iping and the appearance of a guest in the winter season is something unheard of. Mrs Hall, the owner of the inn, is delighted to have a guest at this time of the year. And she makes him some supper and goes to his room. Though the fire was on, the man still persisted in keeping himself covered. Mrs Hall asks him to take the coat and the hat off but he refuses.

The Strange Appearance of the Visitor

The next time Mrs Hall saw the stranger, he had his over-coat and hat removed. Mrs Hall met a ghastly sight that made her heart skip a beat. The stranger's forehead above his blue glasses was covered by a white bandage. His hair escaping through the bandages looked like tails and horns, giving him the most unimaginable appearance.

The Strange Man's Arrival

आइपिंग में अजनबी का आना

कहानी का प्रारंभ एक Stranger (अजनबी) के Bramblehurst (ब्रेम्बलहस्ट) रेलवे स्टेशन पर पहुँचने से होता है। फरवरी का महीना था और बर्फबारी का तूफान पूरे जोरों पर था। सिर से लेकर पैर तक उसने अपने आप को ढक रखा था, केवल उसकी गुलाबी नाक दिख रही थी। उसने नीले रंग का एक चश्मा भी पहन रखा था। वह एक सराय, जिसका नाम था 'Coach and Horses' (कोच एण्ड हॉर्सेज) में गया और कमरे के लिए पूछा।

अजनबी के आइपिंग आने का असामान्य समय

Iping (आइपिंग) में कँपा देने वाली सर्दी पड़ रही थी तथा ऐसे समय में किसी अतिथि का आना थोड़ा अजीब था। वर्ष के इस समय में किसी ग्राहक को देखकर, सराय की मालकिन, Mrs Hall (मिसेज हॉल) प्रसन्न हो गई। मिसेज हॉल ने उसे उसका कमरा दिखाया और उसके लिए खाने का इंतजाम किया। उसके कमरे में आग जल रही थी, परंतु आदमी ने अपने आपको ढक रखा था। मिसेज हॉल ने उससे अपना कोट व टोपी उतारने को कहा, परंतु उसने मना कर दिया।

अजनबी का अजीबोगरीब दिखना

अगली बार जब मिसेज हॉल ने अजनबी को देखा, उस समय वह अपना कोट और टोपी उतार चुका था। मिसेज हॉल ने एक डरावना दृश्य देखा, जिसे देखकर वह सन्न रह गई। अजनबी के सिर का नीले चश्में से ऊपर का हिस्सा एक सफेद पट्टी से ढका हुआ था। उसके बाल पट्टियों में से बाहर आते हुए किसी पूँछ व सींग की तरह लग रहे थे, जिसके कारण वह अत्यंत अजीब लग रहा था।

The Stranger Finally Talks

Mrs Hall perceived that probably the visitor had a very bad accident and that had disfigured his face. Mrs Hall felt sorry for him. The time Mrs Hall went to clear his lunch, the stranger finally talks to her. He asks if his luggage could be brought from the station that very day. Mrs Hall replies in the negative. Mrs Hall initiates more talks, but then he abruptly tells her to bring some matches. Mrs Hall thinks that it was quite rude of him. But then, she thought of the rent and went away.

अजनबी ने अंत में बात की

मिसेज हॉल ने महसूस किया कि शायद अजनबी ने एक भयंकर दुर्घटना को करीब से महसूस किया है, जिसके कारण उसका चेहरा खराब हो गया है। मिसेज हॉल को उसके लिए खेद हुआ। जब मिसेज हॉल उसका खाना खत्म होने के बाद उससे मिलने आई तब अजनबी ने उससे बात की। उसने पूछा कि क्या रेलवे स्टेशन से उसका सामान उसी दिन आ सकता है। मिसेज हॉल ने नकारात्मक उत्तर दिया। मिसेज हॉल उससे अत्यधिक बातें करना चाहती थी, परंतु उसने उससे एकाएक कुछ माचिसें मँगाईं। मिसेज हॉल को उसका कठोर व्यवहार बहुत अजीब लगा। परंतु किराये के रूप में मिलने वाले धन के बारे में सोचकर वह चुप रह गई।

Word Meaning

Wrapped	– लिपटा हुआ	Brim	– ऊपर तक
Crest	– चोटी	Staggered	– लड़खड़ाना
Charity	– दया	Sovereigns	– ब्रिटिश सिक्के
Resolved	– तय होना	Deftly	– बारीकी से
Brisk up	– जोर लगाना	Sprinkled	– छिड़कना
Dripped	– रिसना	Whisked	– जल्दीबाजी में
Promptly	– तेजी से	Glimpse	– झलक
Resolutely	– चालाकी से	Brooked	– मान लेना
Muffled	– चुपचाप	Gaping	– घूर कर देखना
Startled	– चौंक जाना	Scrap	– टुकड़ा
Conceivable	– समझने लायक	Anticipated	– उम्मीद करना
Perplexity	– चिंतित होना	Obscured	– धुंधला
Aggressive	– शत्रुता	Loath	– अनिच्छुक
Jest	– मजाक	Dread	– डरावना
Gasped	– जोर से साँस लेना	Creaked	– चरमराना

Important Questions

Questions based on the Plot of the Chapter

Q 1. Why was Mrs Hall happy to have a visitor?

मिसेज हॉल अतिथि के आने पर खुश क्यों थी?

आइपिंग में व्यक्तियों का गर्मियों में आना – सर्दियों में व्यक्तियों का आइपिंग न जाना – अजनबी वैज्ञानिक का उस गाँव में आना – सबको बड़ी हैरानी होना – मिसेज हॉल का मकान मालकिन होना – उसका खुश होना – उसे व्यापार मिल जाना – अजनबी वैज्ञानिक का मोल-भाव करना, जो आश्चर्यजनक था।

Ans. Iping was such a village that attracted a few folk people during summer, but during winter none visited the village. Scientist, who was a stranger happened to visit the same village. When he reached there, it was an unusual act on the side of a person there. Mrs Hall, who was the landlady, she was very happy because she would be having some business with the strange scientist.

Above all, the scientist was under a bargain even. Mrs Hall could not believe her luck as the idle time was giving her a business.

Q 2. For a moment, Mrs Hall stood gaping at him, too surprised to speak. Why was she surprised?

मिसेज हॉल कुछ देर तक अजनबी को खड़े होकर घूरती रही। उसने ऐसा क्यों किया?

अजनबी का कमरे में आग के सामने आना – मिसेज हॉल से खाने की माँग करना – मिसेज हॉल का खाना लेकर आना – अजनबी का आग के पास खड़ा होना – मिसेज हॉल की आवाज को अनसुना करना – अजनबी का अंत में मुड़ना – मिसेज हॉल का देखना – अजनबी के पूरे चेहरे पर एक पट्टी बँधी होना – मिसेज हॉल का महसूस करना कि एक भयंकर दुर्घटना के कारण उसका चेहरा खराब होना।

Ans. As the stranger entered the room and he went on with warming himself, in between he asked the lady for supper and when the lady arrived with that, he was then standing closer to the fire with the back facing the lady. The lady called him and he didn't turn back. She thought that he had not heard her properly so she called him again. Then the lady stood there gaping at him and when he made a turn. She was surprised as there was bandages only over his face and his face was much disfigured. He was thought to have suffered an accident.

Mr Teddy Henfrey's First Impression

Mr Teddy Henfrey : A Clock Repairer

It was 4' o clock when Mrs Hall was gathering courage to go to the visitor to ask for tea. Meanwhile Mr Teddy Henfrey, a clock-repairer, came into the inn. Mrs Hall takes him to the stranger's room to repair his clock and asks if he wanted some tea.

Mrs Hall opens the door without knocking and in the dim light notices the stranger. She is dazzled to see that the stranger had no lower jaw or had a giant mouth. However, Mrs Hall thinks that the dim lights have deceived her.

The Stranger Asks not to be Disturbed

Mr Teddy Henfrey is taken aback by the ghastly appearance of the stranger. The stranger says that he doesn't like to be disturbed. He further asks Mrs Hall about his luggage and informs the two that he is an experimental investigator. Hence, his luggage is very important. He further tells them that he has come to Iping for solitude.

Mr Teddy Henfrey is Snubbed by the Stranger

Mrs Hall leaves Mr Teddy Henfrey in the stranger's room to fix the clock. Mr Teddy Henfrey takes a long time with the clock on purpose, so that he can see more of the stranger. As soon as he tried to do so, the stranger snubbed him and asked him to finish the work and go.

Mr Teddy Henfrey's First Impression

मि टेडी हेनफ्रे : घड़ी मरम्मत करने वाला

शाम के चार बजे Mrs Hall (मिसेज हॉल) अजनबी से चाय के बारे में पूछने के लिए हिम्मत जुटा रही थी। तभी Mr Teddy Henfrey (मि टेडी हेनफ्रे) घड़ी की मरम्मत करने वाला, सराय में आया। मिसेज हॉल उसे अजनबी के कमरे में घड़ी को ठीक करने के लिए ले गई और उससे चाय के लिए पूछा।

मिसेज हॉल ने बिना खटखटाए दरवाजा खोला और मंद रोशनी में उसने अजनबी को देखा। वह ये देखकर चौंक गई कि अजनबी के न तो मुँह था और न ही निचला जबड़ा। हालाँकि, मिसेज हॉल को लगा कि कमरे की मंद रोशनी ने उसे धोखा दिया है।

अजनबी का शांति भंग न करने के लिए कहना

मि टेडी हेनफ्रे अजनबी के आविर्भाव को देखकर चौंक गया। अजनबी ने कहा कि वह नहीं चाहता कि उसे कोई तंग करे। उसने मिसेज हॉल से अपने सामान के बारे में पूछा और उसने उन दोनों को बताया कि वह एक प्रयोगात्मक जाँच करने वाला (वैज्ञानिक) है। अत: उसके लिए उसका सामान बहुत ही महत्त्वपूर्ण है। उसने यह भी बताया कि वह Iping (आइपिंग) शांति के लिए आया है।

अजनबी का मि टेडी हेनफ्रे को डाँटना

मिसेज हॉल ने घड़ी ठीक करने के लिए मि टेडी हेनफ्रे को अजनबी के कमरे में छोड़ दिया। मि टेडी हेनफ्रे ने घड़ी को ठीक करने में ज्यादा वक्त लगाया, ताकि वह अजनबी को देख सके। जैसे ही उसने ऐसा करने का प्रयास किया अजनबी ने उसे डाँट दिया और जल्द ही काम खत्म करके जाने को कहा।

Mr Teddy Henfrey Meets Mr Hall and Tells him about the Stranger

On his way, Mr Teddy Henfrey thought that the stranger was perhaps wanted by the police. He meets Mr Hall at a crossing. Mr Hall had recently married Mrs Hall. Mr Hall drives a carriage. Mr Teddy Henfrey tells him about the stranger and says that his appearance looks a sort of a disguise.

मि टेडी हेनफ्रे का मि हॉल से मिलने के बाद अजनबी के बारे में बताना

मि टेडी हेनफ्रे रास्ते में यही सोच रहा था कि शायद अजनबी को पुलिस तलाश रही है। रास्ते में वह मि हॉल से मिला। हाल ही Mr Hall (मि हॉल) ने मिसेज हॉल से शादी की थी। मि हॉल एक ताँगा चलाने वाला था। मि टेडी हेनफ्रे ने उसे उस अजनबी के बारे में बताया और कहा उसकी उपस्थिति ऐसी दिखाई देती है जैसे कि वह अपने आप को छिपा रहा हो।

Mr Hall Runs Home and Gets Rebuked

When Mr Hall inquired about the stranger, he got rebuked by his wife for returning home drunk. Mr Hall scrutinised his papers left in the parlour. He asked his wife (Mrs Hall) to search the stranger's luggage the next day. But Mrs Hall him to mind his own business.

घर जाने पर मि हॉल की स्थिति

जब मि हॉल ने अजनबी के बारे में पूछा, तो उसकी पत्नी ने शराब पीकर घर आने के लिए खूब डाँटा। मि हॉल ने बैठक में रखे कुछ दस्तावेजों की जाँच की। उसने अपनी पत्नी (मिसेज हॉल) से अगले दिन अजनबी के सामान की तलाशी लेने को कहा, लेकिन मिसेज हॉल ने उन्हें अपना काम-से-काम रखने के लिए कहा।

Word Meaning

Screwing – इकट्ठा करना
Drooping – नीचे की तरफ झूलता हुआ
Downcast – उदास
Vestiges – बरकरार रहना
Dazzled – उलझन भरा
Incredible – अतुल्य
Monstrous – राक्षसी प्रवृत्ति का
Drowsy – नींद से भरा हुआ
Lobster – एक प्रकार की समुद्री मछली
Anticipation – उम्मीद
Snubbed – डाँट देना
Investigator – जाँच-पड़ताल करने वाला
Baggage – सामान
Appliances – यंत्र/मशीन
Deliberation – सोच-समझकर किया जाना
Excruciating – बहुत ज्यादा दर्दनाक
Irresistible – जिसे रोका न जा सके
Patches – दाग
Proceeding – कार्य-कलाप
Severely rated – बुरे तरीके से पेश आना
Suppressed – दबाया हुआ
Trudging – धीरे-धीरे चलना
Grotesque – बदसूरत
Concerned – लगाव
Apprehension – समझ
Vaguely – अनिश्चित रूप से
Germinated – अंकुरित होना
Scrutinised – बारीकी से जाँचना
Computations – गणनाएँ
Turnip – शलजम
Interminable – कभी समाप्त न होने वाला

Jobber – मरम्मत करने वाला
Adverse – विपरीत
Scanty – सीमित
Ruddy – गुलाबी रंग का
Enormous – पर्याप्त मात्रा से ज्यादा
Swallowed – निगल जाना
Yawn – जम्हाई लेना
Confronted – सामना होना
Apologise – माफी माँगना
Reassured – भरोसा दिलाना
Fatigued – थका होना
Indeed – वास्तव में
Apparatus – औजार
Anxious – उत्सुक
Solitude – शांति
Annoyance – गुस्सा/नाराजगी
Extracted – बाहर निकाला जाना
Constitutionally – प्राकृतिक तौर पर
Uncanny – अजीबोगरीब
Evidently – स्पष्ट तौर पर
Humbugging – धोखा देना
Vivid – अलग-अलग किस्म का
Disguise – छलावा
Sluggish – आलसी
Swindled – धोखा देना
Snappishly – गुस्से से
Ascertain – निश्चय करना
Contemptously – असभ्यता के साथ
Inclined – इरादतन
Trailing – पीछा करना
Subdued – नियंत्रित करना

Important Questions

Questions based on the Plot of the Chapter

Q 1. Why does Mrs Hall ask Mr Teddy Henfrey to repair the clock in the stranger's room?

मिसेज हॉल ने मि टेडी हेनफ्रे को अजनबी के कमरे की घड़ी ठीक करने को क्यों कहा?

मि टेडी हेनफ्रे का जबरदस्त सर्दी में धर्मशाला आना – मिसेज हॉल का इस मौके का फायदा उठाना – मिसेज हॉल के दो निजी स्वार्थ भी इससे जुड़े होना – घड़ी को ठीक कराना – सकारात्मक प्रभाव पड़ना – मिसेज हॉल को व्यापारिक लाभ मिलना – दूसरे स्वार्थ में अजनबी के बारे में पता चलना – मिसेज हॉल को अंदर जाने का एक मौका मिलना – अजनबी को खुश करने का भी अवसर मिलना – अजनबी से चाय के लिए पूछना – उसका असमय यहाँ आना – उसके रहस्यमयी होने का राज मालूम होना।

Ans. Mr Teddy Henfrey came at the inn in the biting cold and Mrs Hall thought to make the opportunity. There were two reasons for it. One was that the clock would be made okay and probably the guest would create a positive apprehension of the most and would advance in the business.

Second one was that with the shadow of Mr Teddy Henfrey, she would enter the room of the stranger and ask him for tea. Even asking for the tea had something to do with the business of Mrs Hall and the curiosity of knowing the stranger completely.

It must be so because the stranger looks always like an awkward man and all his behaviours seemed to be like that. The stranger's face was unknown and it couldn't be revealed yet so far.

He arrived at the village on such a time when no one could expect a visitor in the village and this added to the curiosity of everybody in the whole village. And, that reason is self sufficient in telling that why Mr Teddy Henfrey wanted to enter the room of the stranger by Mrs Hall then.

Q 2. Who is Mr Teddy Henfrey? What was his first reaction when he saw the stranger?

मि टेडी हेनफ्रे कौन था? अजनबी को देखने के बाद उसकी पहली प्रतिक्रिया क्या थी?

मि टेडी हेनफ्रे का आइपिंग गाँव में रहना – मि टेडी हेनफ्रे का घड़ी की मरम्मत करने वाला होना – मि टेडी हेनफ्रे का अपने काम में निपुण होना – मिसेज हॉल की धर्मशाला पर जाना – घड़ी मरम्मत करने के दौरान अजनबी पर शक होना – मि टेडी हेनफ्रे का सोचना कि अजनबी पुलिस से भागा हुआ एक अपराधी है – मि टेडी हेनफ्रे की जिज्ञासा का चरम सीमा पर होना – हर हाल में कुछ जानकारी लेने की कोशिश करना।

Ans. Mr Teddy Henfrey was a resident of the Iping village. Mr Teddy Henfrey was a clock-jobber and he used to earn his living by doing this. When he reached the inn of Mrs Hall, he was told that the clock in the parlour had not been working properly. He was to repair that, he entered the room of the stranger and as he entered, he got the very first surprise on seeing the stranger. His first reaction was that the man must have been a convict and police was chasing him. To save himself from the police, he had hid himself here and had a bandaged face. It was very obvious that even if Mr Teddy Henfrey was a clock-jobber and his earning was very meagre, he had got some sense of real mechanic. A real mechanic must be nosey and inquisitive because it helped in his profession. Such helpful tendencies were there in him as he was delaying his work consciously just because of the fact that he wanted to know something about the stranger. He even tried to start the conversation with him so that something might come as an output of his inquisitiveness.

Q 3. What did the stranger tell Mrs Hall about his behaviour?

अजनबी ने मिसेज हॉल को अपने व्यवहार के बारे में क्या बताया?

अजनबी का अजीबोगरीब व्यवहार करना – किसी के लिए भी एक उत्सुकता – हर किसी का उससे बात करना – उसके बारे में जानने की इच्छा रखना – मिसेज हॉल को एक दिन मौका मिलना – अजनबी द्वारा अपने सामान के बारे में पूछना – मिसेज हॉल का उसको बताना कि एक या दो दिन और लगेंगे – अपने व्यवहार के बारे में अजनबी द्वारा कहना – एक दुर्घटना के बाद से उसके स्वभाव में और चेहरे में बदलाव आना – उसको किसी से भी बात करना अच्छा न लगना।

Ans. As the stranger was packed with the strange and odd behaviours so he was the most desired in the locality. Everybody was keen and curious about pinning some knowledge and some information about him so that they might understand the stranger. Mrs Hall, therefore didn't miss any moment to have a chance of visiting her guest and thus, she was looking for a chance to be with him. One fine day, she got that opportunity to have a nice and friendly talk with him. She was asked by the stranger that when he could expect his luggages to arrive at the inn.

Mrs Hall let him know that it would take a day or two to reach here. The stranger also allowed her to know that an accident has defaced him and now he looked so ugly and that's why he had to cover his face with bandages and all that. Mrs Hall gave her consent to him recalling the accident of one of her relatives. The stranger also told her that now he didn't want anyone to talk to him more and it was the accident that had made his behaviour awkward.

Q 4. Mr Hall was suspicious about the stranger. Comment.

मि हॉल उस अजनबी मेहमान के बारे में ज्यादा से ज्यादा क्यों जानना चाहते थे?

मि टेडी हेनफ्रे की जिज्ञासा – वार्तालाप द्वारा अजनबी के बारे में पता करने की कोशिश करना – अजनबी द्वारा मि टेडी हेनफ्रे को समय खराब करते हुए पकड़ लेना – मि टेडी हेनफ्रे को लगना कि अजनबी पुलिस से छिप रहा है – धर्मशाला छोड़ने पर मि टेडी हेनफ्रे की रास्ते में मि हॉल से मुलाकात होना – मि टेडी हेनफ्रे द्वारा मि हॉल को बताना – अपराधी का उसकी धर्मशाला में निवास करना – मि हॉल का उस अपराधी के बारे में मिसेज हॉल से पूछना – मिसेज हॉल द्वारा मि हॉल को डाँट मिलना – मि हॉल का शक गहरा होना – उसका तय करना कि वह अपराधी के बारे में और पता लगाएगा।

Ans. The story reveals that the most inquisitive person was Mr Teddy Henfrey, the clock-jobber. He was the first, if not the first, the second who got the chance to see the stranger closely. During his job of repairing the clock, he was putting more time so that he might get a chance to start the conversation with him. When he failed in doing this and got caught by the stranger that he was wasting his time, he made a feeling that the man must be a convict and police was behind him. In order to save himself from the police, he had been hiding here.

When he left the inn, he met Mr Hall on the way. Mr Hall was driving his cart then. Mr Teddy Henfrey told him the whole story about the stranger and put up his speculation before him that he must be a convict. Mr Hall was carried away by the words of Mr Teddy Henfrey and as he reached his home being drunk, he started to question his wife about the stranger but Mr Hall was rebuked by his wife. After that, Mr Hall resolved that he would try and find out who the stranger was and it was a resolution.

Question based on the Character Sketch

Q 5. What impression do you form about Mr Teddy Henfrey after reading this chapter?

इस पाठ को पढ़ने के बाद मि टेडी हेनफ्रे के बारे में आपकी क्या राय बनती है?

मि टेडी हेनफ्रे का अपना काम बखूबी जानना – अजनबी से बात करने की कोशिश करना – अपनी जिज्ञासा शांत करने की कोशिश करना – अजनबी द्वारा डाँटने पर धर्मशाला से चले जाना – उसे पुलिस से भागता हुआ अपराधी बताना – मि हॉल को रास्ते में अजनबी और उसके व्यवहार के बारे में बताना – मि टेडी हेनफ्रे की प्रभावशाली कला द्वारा चीजों को अच्छे से प्रस्तुत करना – मिसेज हॉल को भी अपनी बातों से प्रभावित करना।

Ans. After reading the chapter, it is got to be known that Mr Teddy Henfrey was a nosey and inquisitive person. He knew that his job of clock-jobbing was so easy and less time taking for him and he would have done that very easily. But his nosey attitude brought him to the point of conversation with the man so that he could know something about the stranger. As he was caught, he left the house and found Mr Hall.

He told the whole, a lot of event and mixing his own elements of fantasy to Mr Hall. He made Mr Hall so deliberate that he was resolved to find out the facts about him. His apprehensions about him was such that everyone could believe him without slightest of doubt in one's own mind.

This proves that Mr Teddy Henfrey was a better orator and preacher too. Also, he put up several evidences for his saying so that one could be taken into his faith of his being true and never doubt on him. Mr Teddy Henfrey gave the same impression to Mrs Hall when he was with her at the inn and why he was saying such and such was totally justified to the lady even. This was his inner talent by far and large.

The Thousand and One Bottles

A Dog Attacks the Stranger

The next day the stranger's luggage arrived at the inn. It was a remarkable luggage. It had six trunks and with them there were big fat books. A dozen or more crates and cases containing objects packed in straw. The cart driver, Fearenside and Mr Hall were talking when the stranger came running for his luggage. At that very instant, Fearenside's dog jumped at the stranger. The dog tore off the glove and the trouser of the stranger.

Mr Hall Gets a Hurt

The stranger rushed into the inn. Mr Hall went to the inn and he entered the stranger's room without announcing himself. The room was dim. He saw something coming towards him, but Mr Hall couldn't make out what it was.

The Stranger Gets Working

The stranger came down. He had changed his trousers and gloves. As soon as the first box was bought in the parlour, the stranger began to unpack. There were bottles of all shapes and sizes in all of the crates.

The Thousand and One Bottles

अजनबी पर कुत्ते का हमला

अगले दिन Stranger (अजनबी) का सामान Inn (सराय) में आ गया। यह एक अद्भुत सामान था। इसमें छः बक्से और इसके अतिरिक्त बड़ी-बड़ी तथा मोटी-मोटी किताबें थीं। एक दर्जन से भी ज्यादा Crates (क्रेट्स) थीं जिनमें घास-फूँस में पैक वस्तुएँ थीं। बग्घी वाला Fearenside (फियरेनसाइड) और मि हॉल आपस मे बात कर रहे थे, तभी अचानक अजनबी अपने सामान के लिए भागता हुआ वहाँ पर आया। उसी क्षण, फियरेनसाइड का कुत्ता अजनबी के ऊपर कूद पड़ा। कुत्ते ने अजनबी के दस्ताने तथा पायजामा फाड़ दिया था।

मि हॉल को चोट पहुँचना

अजनबी सराय की ओर भागा। मि हॉल भी सराय की ओर गए और अजनबी की अनुमति के बिना ही मि हॉल उसके कमरे में चले गए, कमरे में अँधेरा था। उसने अपनी तरफ आते हुए कुछ देखा परंतु मि हॉल को समझ नहीं आया कि वह चीज क्या थी।

अजनबी का काम में लगना

अजनबी नीचे आया। उसने अपने दस्ताने और पायजामा बदल रखा था। जैसे ही पहला बक्सा बैठक में आया अजनबी ने उसे खोलना शुरू कर दिया। बक्से में अलग-अलग किस्म की छोटी-बड़ी बोतलें थीं।

Mrs Hall Again Experiences Something Obscure

The stranger was engrossed in his work. He was so busy that he didn't hear Mrs Hall knocking or even coming in. Mrs Hall thought that his eye sockets were hollow. The stranger complained that he was being disturbed. Mrs Hall asked him to lock the door.

मिसेज हॉल को पुन: संदेह का आभास होना

अजनबी अपने काम में व्यस्त हो गया। अजनबी काम में इतना व्यस्त था कि उसे दरवाजे पर मिसेज हॉल की दस्तक या उनके आने का भी कोई ध्यान नहीं रहा। मिसेज हॉल को ऐसा लगा कि उसकी आँखों के गड्डे खाली हैं। अजनबी ने कहा कि वह उसे परेशान कर रही है। मिसेज हॉल ने उसे दरवाजा बंद रखने के लिए कहा।

Word Meaning

Thaw – बर्फबारी
Rational – हकीकत के अनुसार
Preparatory – शुरूआती
Dilettante – पेशेवर
Growl – गुर्राना
Sprang – कूदना या छलांग लगाना
Rip – फटना
Dismay – चिंता
Stoop – झुका हुआ
Indeterminate – अनिश्चित
Concussion – झटका
Fatuities – बेवकूफी
Inflamed – प्रज्वलित करना
Swore – गंदे शब्द
Fluted – लंबी धारीदार
Bungs – डाल देना
Hollow – खाली
Slush – कीचड़ व बर्फ के बीच
Impatiently – बेचैनी
Sniffing – सूँघना
Bristle – गुस्से से दूर खड़े होना
Savagely – निर्दयता से
Flanking – किनारे-किनारे
Yelping – चिल्लाना
Retreated – निर्णय बदलना
Trotted – धीरे-धीरे चलना
Pale Pansy – एक प्रकार का फूल
Forge – भट्ठी
Incredible – अतुल्य
Anonymous – बेनाम
Slender – दुबला-पतला
Frosted – जमा हुआ
Chiffonnier – ढाँचा
Exasperation – निराशा

Important Questions

Question based on the Plot of the Chapter

Q 1. Mr Hall saw something he could not comprehend. Comment.

मि हॉल ने कुछ ऐसा देखा, जो वह समझ नहीं पाए। टिप्पणी करें।

↗ अजनबी का अपने सामान के लिए बेचैन होना – मि हॉल से बार-बार सामान को कहना – एक दिन उसका सामान आना – खुशी से अजनबी का अपने सामान के लिए नीचे आना – बग्घी के पास कुत्ते द्वारा अजनबी के पैरों पर काटना – अजनबी का अपने कमरे में कपड़े बदलने के लिए जाना – मि हॉल का अजनबी के पीछे हाल-चाल पूछने जाना – मि हॉल का बिना अनुमति के कमरे में प्रवेश करना – पीटने के बाद दरवाजा बंद करना – मि हॉल को समझ न आना कि उसको किसने पीटा।

Ans. The impatience of the stranger was at the sky high, when he was waiting for all his luggage to arrive there. He had repeatedly told Mr Hall about his luggage, but it was an outcome for the delay. As he was much worried about all his belongings so he was getting much frustrated. Finally, he received it one day and his happiness had no limit. He just went down and started unloading the stuffs and then unpacking it.

But before that when he was standing near the coach for his luggage, just that moment a dog had bitten him on his legs.

It was due to the fact that he was a stranger and was behaving in the same fashion then. The dog's bite hurt him and he ran towards his room to change his trousers so that he may avoid any of further suspicion.

Mr Hall followed the stranger just because of asking if he was fine. He entered in the same flow to the stranger's room. The stranger beat him mercilessly and then door was slammed behind Mr Hall. Mr Hall could not understand who had beaten him this way and who had closed the door as there was none in the room then.

Mr Cuss Interviews the Stranger

Money Keeps Mrs Hall Mum

Not much happened in Iping until the Club Festival. The stranger kept having small issues with Mrs Hall over his domestic demeanour, but he always shut her up by asking her to bill him extra.

The Stranger is Alone

The stranger never went to church and liked to live alone. He worked very fitfully. His behaviour was always unpredictable and he was also violent sometimes. He had no communication with the outside world and rarely went out in broad daylight.

The Stranger is the Talk of the Town

The stranger had become the talk of the town. Mrs Hall defended him by telling that her guest was an 'experimental investigator' and Mrs Hall explained the people that he had an accident which temporarily discoloured his face and hands. Some thought that he was a criminal. Then there were talks of him being a piebald, but all of Iping disliked him.

4

Mr Cuss Interviews the Stranger

धन की वजह से मिसेज हॉल का चुप रहना

Club Festival (क्लब फेस्टिवल) तक Iping (आइपिंग) में कुछ खास नहीं हुआ। अजनबी को अपने घरेलू व्यवहार के कारण Mrs Hall (मिसेज हॉल) के साथ छोटी-छोटी समस्याएँ तो थीं, परंतु वह हमेशा उसे अतिरिक्त भुगतान देने को कहकर शांत कर दिया करता था।

अजनबी का अकेला होना

अजनबी कभी भी चर्च नहीं गया और वह अकेला रहना पसंद करता था। वह बहुत ही लगन से काम करता था। उसके व्यवहार के बारे में कुछ भी कहना अनिश्चित था और वह कभी-कभी हिंसक भी हो जाता था। बाहरी दुनिया से उसका कोई संपर्क नहीं था और दिन में वह शायद ही कभी बाहर निकलता था।

अजनबी का पूरे शहर में चर्चा का विषय होना

अजनबी पूरे शहर में चर्चा का विषय बन चुका था। मिसेज हॉल अजनबी का पक्ष लेते हुए कहती है कि वह एक 'वैज्ञानिक' है और मिसेज हॉल ने लोगों को बताया कि एक दुर्घटना के कारण उसका चेहरा और हाथ चितकबरे हो गए हैं। कुछ लोग समझते थे कि वह एक अपराधी है। उसके मिले हुए रंगों (चितकबरा) का व्यक्ति होने की चर्चाएँ थीं, परंतु आइपिंग के सभी लोग उसे नापसंद करते थे।

Mr Cuss' Curiousness

Mr Cuss, the general practitioner, was very much interested in the stranger. He wanted to know why the man possessed one thousand and one bottles. He used the excuse of a nurse fund and visited the stranger and Mr Cuss got chance to talk to the strange man.

While the two men were talking, Mrs Hall stood outside and tried to hear what was happening. She heard a cry of surprise, then a curious laughter and then Mr Cuss appeared. No sooner that he had appeared, Mr Cuss ran across the hall and right down the road.

मि कस की उत्सुकता

Mr Cuss (मि कस), जो वहाँ के चिकित्सक थे, को अजनबी के बारे में जानने की बड़ी उत्सुकता थी। वे जानना चाहते थे कि उसके पास एक हजार एक बोतल क्यों हैं। वह Nurse Fund (नर्स फंड) के लिए चंदा लेने का बहाना बनाकर अजनबी के पास गए और मि कस को उस अजनबी व्यक्ति से बात करने का अवसर मिला।

जब वे दोनों बात कर रहे थे, उस समय मिसेज हॉल बाहर खड़ी थी और सुनने की कोशिश कर रही थी कि क्या हो रहा था। उसने एक आश्चर्य भरा रोना सुना, फिर हँसी और फिर मि कस कमरे से निकलकर आए। जैसे ही वह दिखाई दी, मि कस कमरे से निकलकर हॉल से होते हुए सड़क की ओर भागे।

A Most Remarkable Story

Mr Cuss went straight to Mr Bunting, the vicar. Mr Bunting thought that Mr Cuss had gone mad. Mr Cuss started narrating the things that he had just seen. He told Mr Bunting that the stranger was a man of irritable temper.

एक कौतूहल भरी कहानी

मि कस भागते हुए पादरी Mr Bunting (मि बंटिंग) के पास गए। मि बंटिंग ने समझा कि मि कस पागल हो गया है। मि कस ने उन चीजों का वर्णन करना शुरू कर दिया, जो उसने अभी-अभी देखी थीं। उसने मि बंटिंग को बताया कि अजनबी एक गुस्से वाला इंसान है।

Word Meaning

Curiously	– उत्सुकतापूर्वक	Skirmishes	– तर्क-वितर्क
Penury	– गरीबी	Expedient	– माप
Concealing	– छिपाना	Ostentatiously	– दिखावापूर्ण
Sagely	– बुद्धिमानी से	Fretting	– चिंतित
Unendurable	– बर्दाश्त के बाहर	Provocation	– उकसाना
Snapped	– टूटना	Spasmodic	– अनियमित
Gusts	– उमंगें	Chronic	– अनवरत
Bogies	– डब्बा	Conscientiously	– बारीकी से
Gingerly	– सावधानी से	Inevitable	– जिसे मना न किया जा सके
Disposition	– हालात	Adverse	– प्रतिकूल
Anarchist	– अराजक	Waverers	– हिचकने वाला
Superstitions	– अंधविश्वास	Frantic	– गुस्सा
Gesticulations	– धमकी भरा	Extinction	– गायब होना
Lunatic	– पागल	Occult	– छिपा हुआ
Tremulously	– हिलाते हुए	Elated	– खुशी से भरा हुआ

Important Questions

Question based on the Plot of the Chapter

Q 1. Why was the stranger the talk of the town?

अजनबी पूरे शहर के लिए चर्चा का विषय क्यों था?

सर्दियों के मौसम में अजनबी का आइपिंग में आना – अजनबी का चेहरा बदनुमा होना – उसका अपने चेहरे पर हमेशा पट्टी लगाकर रखना – उसका गुस्सैल स्वभाव का होना – लोगों का साथ उसे पसंद न होना – उसका बहुत ही असामाजिक होना – अपने काम में किसी तरह की दखलअंदाजी पसंद न करना – उसका कभी चर्च न जाना – लोगों का उसे अपराधी समझना – इन सबकी वजह से वह चर्चा का विषय था।

Ans. The stranger arrived at the Iping village at a time when no visitor was expected to arrive there. It was the time of biting and chilly cold when Iping was never a suitable place to see, then the visitor made his appearance there. This made many a mouths open wide. Another thing was the fact that his face was disfigured and people couldn't see his face very clearly. He always wore bandages and all that stuffed to cover his face. That made the people fall in surprise. Next thing, that was an oddity with him, was his nature.

He was a short-tempered man and got easily irritated even when a person was trying to be a bit social with him.

He didn't like the company of other persons. Most of the interesting fact about him was that he never wanted to get disturbed by anyone in his work ever. He didn't like to go to the church and most people had different speculation about him to be a convict or a piebald. All these things made the man a talk of the town. He should certainly do it as these were completely peculiar.

Question based on the Character Sketch

Q 2. What impression do you form about Mr Cuss?

मि कस के बारे में आपकी क्या अवधारणा है?

पाठ के आधार पर मि कस का आइपिंग में सबसे उत्सुक व्यक्ति होना – उनका अजनबी से मिलने के लिए अपनी उत्सुकता न रोक पाना – चंदा लेने की योजना बनाकर अजनबी से मिलने के लिए जाना – मूल उद्देश्य अजनबी के बारे में अपनी जिज्ञासा को शांत करना – बातचीत शुरू करना – अंततः वहाँ से भाग जाना – मि बंटिंग से मिलना और आपबीती बताना – मि बंटिंग की मदद लेना – मि बंटिंग एक ऐसे इंसान, जो तथ्यों को साधारणतया रखना जानते थे।

Ans. On the basis of this chapter, we can thus conclude about Mr Cuss. At first, we must say that he was the man whose curiosity was at the highest and he didn't restrain himself from visiting the stranger. He did it with a meticulous planning.

He planned some funding procedure for the nurse and went to the stranger to share the idea in the hope of getting some fund. But the vital and core motto that was to get acquainted with the stranger was priority.

He at first fell into the conversation but soon the conversation was moulded into a series of shriek, laughter and the fleeing away of Mr Cuss.

Afterwards, he reached Mr Bunting whom he told the whole of the event. He believed that Mr Bunting could be the only one to justify what he had seen there in the inn.

This gives us the impression that he had some irrational thoughts, to seek the assistance of a rational man like Mr Bunting. There was no mixing up of anything in the story as some extra inputs that shows that he was a man who put all the facts plainly and bluntly.

Q 3. On the basis of your reading the chapter attempt a Character-Sketch of Mr Bunting?

इस पाठ के आधार पर मि बंटिंग का चरित्र-चत्रिण करें?

मि बंटिंग चर्च में पादरी थे– आईपिंग में उनकी प्रतिष्ठा थी– सीधे-साधे तथा आकर्षक व्यक्तित्त्व के स्वामी थे– चीजों को यथार्थता की कसौटी पर रखने के बाद ही स्वीकार करते करते थे– उनके ज्ञान की वजह से लोग उनकी राय लेते वे मदगार इंसान थे– एक उच्चतम कोटि के चरित्र थे।

Ans. Iping has been a place where folks of all kinds live harmonically and with uniformity. He was the vicar at 10 cal church and due to his prestigious position and his wisdom everybody respected him. He was a man of simplicity and some austere principles and his reputation was sry high.

He was loved by all as he listened to everybody. His thoughts were rational and pragmatic too. When Mr. cuss was beaten up by some mysterious figure then be went to Mr Bunting straight way as he was aware of the fact that only he could be able to solve the mystery of this invisibility.

The chapter reveals that Mr Bunting was a resourceful man and of high dignity. He was very helpful in the affairs of others. In short, he was a great personality and the iconic figure in the whole Iping.

The Burglary at the Vicarage

The Bunting's Family are Awaken

The day was about to come up when Mrs Bunting was suddenly awoken. She thought that perhaps the door of their bedroom was opened and closed. Then she heard the sounds of someone's footsteps. She made sure that a burglar was at work before awaking her husband up. Mr Bunting armed himself with the poker and descended the staircase noiselessly. It was around four in the morning. Mr Bunting moved towards the study room cautiously. Then they heard the chink of money and realising that the burglar had found the gold coins, Mr Bunting searched for the burglar into the room. They searched a lot, but their money also was not there.

बंटिंग परिवार का जाग जाना

सुबह लगभग होने ही वाली थी कि Mrs Bunting (मिसेज बंटिंग) अचानक नींद से जाग गई। उसे लगा कि शायद उसके बेडरूम का दरवाजा खुला और बंद हो गया। उसके बाद उसे किसी के पैरों की आवाज सुनाई दी। उसने अपने पति को जगाने से पहले यह निश्चित कर लिया कि घर में कोई चोर है। Mr Bunting (मि बंटिंग) ने अपने हाथ में एक डण्डा उठाया और दबेपाँव सीढ़ियों से नीचे उतर गए। सुबह के लगभग चार बज चुके थे। मि बंटिंग अपने पढ़ने वाले कक्ष की तरफ सावधानीपूर्वक बढ़ने लगे। जब उन्होंने सिक्के की आवाज सुनी और उन्हें यह अहसास हुआ कि चोर ने उनके सोने के सिक्के खोज लिए हैं, मि बंटिंग कमरे के अंदर चोर को खोजने लग गए। उन्होंने बहुत खोजा, परंतु उनका धन भी वहाँ नहीं था।

Word Meaning

Burgalry	– चोरी	Vicarage	– पादरी का घर
Devoted	– समर्पित होना	Festivities	– उत्सव
Dawn	– सुबह का समय	Distinctly	– साफ तौर पर
Fumbling	– लड़खड़ाना	Sneeze	– छींकना
Weapon	– हथियार	Poker	– लोहे की रॉड
Tread	– हिलना	Nerved	– मजबूत करना
Kindred	– बराबर का	Flared	– चमक
Quaintly	– अजीब तरीके से		

Important Questions

Question based on the Plot of the Chapter

Q 1. Many unusual things happened in the house at the night of the robbery. Elaborate.

चोरी वाली रात को कई अविश्वसनीय घटनाएँ घटीं। उन घटनाओं का वर्णन करें।

चोरी, एक अजीब घटनाओं का संकलन – बंटिंग परिवार के आश्चर्य की सीमा न होना – मिसेज बंटिंग का अजीब आवाजें सुनकर पति को जगाना – मि बंटिंग का लोहे की रॉड लेकर चोर को खोजना – आवाज की दिशा में जाना, पर किसी का न मिलना – मोमबत्ती का अपने आप जल उठना – पढ़ने वाले कक्ष में टेबल की तह का अपने आप खुल जाना – कागजों की सरकने की आवाज होना।

Ans. Since, the robbery was such an event that left the Buntings deeply surprised and their mouth wide opened. Of course, it was the resultant of the unusual events that were noticed during the process of the strange robbery. At first, when Mrs Bunting heard the sound then she awoke Mr Bunting. He picked an iron-rod in his hand and went in the search of the thief. He was following the direction from where the noise was coming. With all possible efforts and with the ultimate attempts, he searched the thief but none could be located and the sounds were still coming.

Next unusual activity was the burning of the candle by none and it was a great surprise to the couple. They found that the table in their study room opened and papers were rustling, but the act was done by none.

The Furniture That Went Mad

Mr Hall Finds the Door of the Strange Man Ajar

The Hall's family were preparing for the Club Festival and thus they had woken up early in the morning. Mr Hall went back up stairs to get some sarsaparilla. He was astonished to see that the stranger's door was open.

There is No One in the Room

Mrs Hall also came to inspect. On her way up, she heard someone sneeze. Mrs Hall thought that Mr Hall had sneezed but on the other hand, Mr Hall thought that it was her who had sneezed. She took a peep into the stranger's room and heard a sniff behind her neck but Mr Hall was quite far away from her. The couple found the stranger's clothes lying here and there along with his head bandages and the stranger was nowhere to be seen.

The Furniture Comes to Life

Mr and Mrs Hall was thinking that it was quite a curious thing that the room was empty, the bed-clothes gathered themselves and jumped headlong over the bottom rail. Then the stranger's cap sprang up and dashed towards Mrs Hall's face. The other things also started to come to life and then the furniture started attacking the Mr and Mrs Hall. The chair pushed the couple out. Mrs Hall thought that her furniture was haunted by spirits.

6

The Furniture That Went Mad

मि हॉल द्वारा अजनबी का दरवाजा अधखुला देखना

हॉल परिवार अपने Club Festival (क्लब उत्सव) की तैयारी करने के लिए जल्दी जाग गया था। Mr Hall (मि हॉल) कुछ मीठा द्रव लाने के लिए ऊपर की ओर गए। उन्होंने अजनबी का कमरा खुला हुआ देखकर आश्चर्य व्यक्त किया।

कमरे के अंदर कोई भी न होना

Mrs Hall (मिसेज हॉल) भी छानबीन करने के लिए अंदर गई। जब वह ऊपर आ रही थी तब उसने किसी के छींकने की आवाज सुनी। मि और मिसेज हॉल एक-दूसरे के लिए समझ रहे थे कि छींक दोनों में से किसी एक की है। मिसेज हॉल ने अजनबी के कमरे में झाँक कर देखा और अपने गले के पास किसी की साँस को महसूस किया परंतु Mr Hall (मि हॉल) उस समय काफी दूर खड़े थे। जब दोनों अजनबी के कमरे के अंदर चले गए तो देखा कि उसके कपड़े और पट्टियाँ कमरे के चारों ओर बिखरी पड़ी थीं और अजनबी अपने कमरे में नहीं था।

कमरे के फर्नीचर का जीवित हो उठना

मि और मिसेज हॉल को अजनबी के कमरे के खाली होने पर बेहद आश्चर्य हो रहा था, तभी बिस्तर पर पड़े कपड़े व सामान अपने आप रहस्यमयी तरीके से जमा हो गए और अपने आप बिस्तर से नीचे आने लगे। उसके बाद अजनबी की टोपी अपने आप हवा में आ गई और मिसेज हॉल के चेहरे पर जा लगी। कमरे में रखा फर्नीचर भी लगभग जीवित हो उठा और मि हॉल तथा मिसेज हॉल के ऊपर जा लगा। कुर्सी ने धक्का मारकर दोनों को कमरे के बाहर कर दिया। मिसेज हॉल को लगा कि उसके फर्नीचर में भूतों का वास हो गया है।

Hall Family Calls for Help

Hall family sent for Mr Sandy Wedgers, the blacksmith. He was a resourceful man. He took a serious view of the situation. Mr Huxter and his apprentice were next to join. Mr Sandy Wedgers himself didn't believe in what the Hall family was saying and wanted to get his facts right.

हॉल परिवार द्वारा मदद के लिए बुलाना

हॉल परिवार ने मि Mr Sandy Wedgers (मि सैंडी वेजर्स), जो एक लोहार थे, उसको बुलाया। वे एक समझदार इंसान थे। उन्होंने स्थिति का सही मूल्यांकन किया। Mr Huxter (मि हक्सटर) और उनका सहयोगी भी वहाँ पर मदद के लिए आ गए। मि सैंडी वेजर्स ने हॉल परिवार की कहानी पर यकीन करने से इंकार कर दिया और अपने स्तर से तथ्यों की सच्चाई का पता लगाने का निश्चय किया।

The Stranger Suddenly Appears

Then suddenly the stranger appeared from his room. No one had seen him until then. He came down and was staring at the gathered party. He rudely slams the door on their faces. Mr Sandy Wedgers told Mr Hall to ask for an explanation. Mr Hall gathered some courage and went to confront him but the stranger shouted and demanded to be left alone.

अजनबी का अचानक प्रकट हो जाना

इन सब के बीच अचानक अजनबी अपने कमरे से बाहर निकल आया। इससे पहले उसे किसी ने नहीं देखा था। वह नीचे आया और बाहर खड़ी भीड़ को घूरकर देखने लगा। उसने दरवाजे को जोर के धक्के के साथ बंद कर दिया। मि सैंडी वेजर्स ने मि हॉल को उससे स्पष्टीकरण माँगने को कहा, तो उसने साहस करके अजनबी से पूछा। अजनबी ने मि हॉल को जोर से डाँटा और अकेला छोड़ने के लिए कहा।

Word Meaning

Ajar	– थोड़ा-सा खुला होना	Latch	– सिटकनी
Rapped	– धक्का मारना	Ascertained	– निश्चय करना
Fancied	– कल्पना करना	Leapt	– उछलना
Clutched	– पकड़ना	Flung	– फेंकना
Whirling	– घूमते हुए	Singularly	– खास का
Screamed	– चीखना	Impelled	– मजबूर करना
Executing	– शुरू करना	Triumph	– जीत
Fainting	– बेहोशी की अवस्था	Restorative	– टॉनिक

Important Questions

Questions based on the Plot of the Chapter

Q 1. What was the Hall couple preparing for? What did they notice in the stranger's room?

हॉल परिवार किस चीज की तैयारी में जुटा था? उन्होंने अजनबी के कमरे में क्या देखा?

आइपिंग का एक उत्सव प्रधान जगह होना – हॉल परिवार का उत्सव की तैयारी करना – एक मीठे द्रव को भूल जाना – मि हॉल का उस द्रव को लाने के लिए ऊपर जाना – अजनबी के कमरे को खुला देखकर आश्चर्य होना – मि और मिसेज हॉल का कमरे के अंदर प्रवेश करना – बिस्तर पर अजनबी के सारे कपड़े और पट्टियाँ नजर आना – बिस्तर का बहुत ही ठंडा होना – अजनबी का बहुत पहले बिस्तर से उठकर जाना – अजीबोगरीब घटना का होना – हॉल परिवार का बहुत आश्चर्यचकित होना।

Ans. Iping was a place that was readily hospitable and a lot of festivities could be seen going on there. It was also the time of festivals when Mr and Mrs Hall were preparing for the same.

They were preparing some soft drinks for that festive occasion and during the night they were busy with that. They had forgotten to carry sarsaparilla with them and that was an ingredient needed in the preparation of that drink.

Mr Hall was asked to carry that one from the up stairs and as he went up, an amazing sight was seen by him. He saw that the room of the stranger was open and the doors were ajar.

Mr Hall called his betterhalf soon and both of them entered the room to see what does it look like from inside. They happened to see that the stranger was not in his room and all his clothes along with the bandages were lying on the bed.

The bed was cold indicating that it's been long since strange man had left his bed. They were amazed to see all these as they had never got a chance to see the room and they had not dared to ask him let them do so even.

Q 2. Who was Sandy Wedgers? What were his views regarding the furniture incident?

सैंडी वेजर्स कौन थे? फर्नीचर वाली घटना के संबंध में उनकी क्या राय थी?

↗ फर्नीचर का रहस्यमय तरीके से जीवित होना – हॉल परिवार का मानना कि फर्नीचर में आत्मा का प्रवेश है – मदद के लिए मि वेजर्स को बुलाना – आत्माओं के साथ पेश आना – हॉल परिवार के द्वारा मि सैंडी वेजर्स को अपनी कहानी को विस्तार से बताना – समझदार इंसान का होना – मि सैंडी वेजर्स का कहानी पर यकीन न करना – अपने स्तर से तथ्यों की सच्चाई का पता लगाना – मि वेजर्स द्वारा मामले की खुद से जाँच-पड़ताल करने का फैसला लेना।

Ans. The event that took place on the eve of the festival was really mysterious. Halls had seen the room of the stranger and they had witnessed such an appalling reality that they could never forget. They saw the furniture of their room going alive and it was thrown over them. They thought that their house was haunted by the spirits. In order to get rid of those spirits, they called Mr Sandy Wedgers. He was the one who used to deal with those spirits in the village Iping. He was a resourceful man and he had been successful in solving the cases like that many a times in his life. When he arrived there, Halls told him their story of the incident they had seen, but Mr Sandy Wedgers was not going to take the story to be true in any case. He told them that he would analyse the whole story on his own accord and then he would say something about the case.

Question based on the Character Sketch

Q 3. The strange man comes about as a man suffering from insanity. What proof do you find in the text to justify the statement?

अजनबी ने लगभग पागलपन-सा दिखाया था। इस पाठ के आधार पर आप इस कथन को कैसे साबित करेंगे?

↗ अजनबी का शुरू से ही रहस्यात्मक होना – उसका पहनावा व दिखावा सामान्य से भिन्न होना – उसके चेहरे का बदनुमा होना व कोई नाक न होना – चेहरे के चारों तरफ पट्टी लगी होना – उसका असामान्य व्यवहार – उसका असामाजिक होना – किसी से न मिलना और न ही बात करना – घरेलू संस्कार की कमी होना – मि हॉल को भी जबदस्त डाँट लगाना – अजनबी का पागलपन दिखना।

Ans. From the very first day, the stranger was the talk of the town. Everybody was curious about him. His curiousity reached its peak. He appeared to be a strange man with all the strange properties in him. His face was disfigured and there was no nose. His face was always covered by bandages all around it. But, the most striking oddity he had was his behaviour. He was never social and friendly. If someone tried to talk to him, he got too infuriated and nobody dared talking him.

When he lacked domestic etiquettes and told that she should add all the damages into his bill, he did not mind anything rude, he had ever done. He always wanted himself to be left alone. After the furniture event when Mr Hall asked for the explanation, he rebuked him severely and it had revealed that how rogue he was! For sure he was a man of science but he was suffering from insanity and he had never won a bit of trust from anyone.

Q 4. Justify sandy wedgers as a resourceful man.

सैंडी वेजर्स को एक साधन संपन्न व्यक्ति के तौर पर सिद्ध कीजए।

आइपिंग में सैंडी वेजर्स एक लोहार थे – कुशल तथा परिश्रमी व्यक्ति थे – अनुभव की पर्याप्तता थी – आइपिंग में उनके अनुभव के कायल कई लोग थे – वे साहसी तथा वैचारिकता से परिपूर्ण व्यक्ति थे – किसी भी नई चीज का बारीकी से अध्ययन करते थे।

Ans. The whole Iping was resourceful is a sense as it has housed people of all virtue and all discipline. Out of the society there was a man named sandy wedgers who was the blacksmith of the village. As his profession needs a hard work so he was really meticulous. He was very amiable to all and due to his submissive nature he was a very popular figure in Iping. He was loved by all. He was having the quality of a patient listener who would listen to everybody. His experience mattered the most is the village. When the fiasco of the stranger came in the village then he was called on the spot so that he could put in his expertise and something could be deduced. He believed in complete rationality and that was his nature. He asserted Mr Hall to enquire about the sudden arrival of the strange man that showed he wished to get all his facts. very right.

The Unveiling of the Stranger

Mrs Hall Decides not to Serve the Stranger

Mrs Hall had decided not to serve the stranger. The stranger kept ringing the bell. By this time, the news of the burglary at the vicarage had spread and everyone suspected the stranger to be the culprit.

The Stranger Comes Out

The stranger was unable to bear the hunger and finally came out. He called for Mrs Hall. Mrs Hall was in a fierce mood. The stranger asked why his breakfast was not laid and Mrs Hall kept asking him to clear his bills.

Mrs Hall Demands an Explanation

Mrs Hall tells him that she wonders where he suddenly got the money from. Mrs Hall wanted to know and everybody else wanted to know what the stranger had done to her chairs and how he appears and disappears without anyone noticing him.

The Stranger Becomes Headless

The stranger pulled out his fake nose and gradually removed all his bandages in front of the them. The crowd was watching this scene. He became headless. Everybody started to run out of the fear. Everyone came out on the street and started talking about what had just happened.

The Unveiling of the Stranger

मिसेज हॉल का अजनबी को खाना नहीं देने का फैसला

Mrs Hall (मिसेज हॉल) ने अजनबी को खाना नहीं देने का फैसला कर लिया। अजनबी लगातार घंटी बजाता रहा। इस समय तक Vicar (पादरी) के घर हुई चोरी का पता चल गया और प्रत्येक व्यक्ति को संदेह था कि चोरी अजनबी ने ही की है।

अजनबी का बाहर आना

भूख से बेहाल होने के बाद अंततः अजनबी अपने कमरे से बाहर आया। उसने मिसेज हॉल को बुलाया। मिसेज हॉल क्रोध में थी। अजनबी ने पूछा कि उसका नाश्ता क्यों नहीं लगाया गया, जिस पर मिसेज हॉल ने उसे अपना बिल चुकाने को कहा।

मिसेज हॉल का अजनबी से स्पष्टीकरण माँगना

मिसेज हॉल ने अजनबी से पूछा कि उसके पास अचानक पैसे कहाँ से आए। मिसेज हॉल व वहाँ पर सभी लोग जानना चाहते थे कि उसने अपनी कुर्सियों के साथ क्या किया है तथा बिना किसी के ध्यान गए वह किस प्रकार आता जाता है।

अजनबी का सिर गायब हो जाना

अजनबी ने अपनी नकली नाक हटा दी और धीरे-धीरे अपने चेहरे पर से पट्टियाँ भी हटा दीं। भीड़ उस दृश्य को देख रही थी। उसका सिर गायब हो गया। सब लोगों ने डर से भागना शुरू कर दिया। सब लोग बाहर सड़को पर आ गए और उस घटना का जिक्र करने लगे।

Bobby Jaffers Comes to Arrest the Stranger

Mr Bobby Jaffers, the village constable, came to arrest the stranger. The people told him about what happened in the inn. Mr Jaffers was resolute and said that head or no head, he had to arrest the man. Mr Jaffers goes in with Mr Hall and Mr Sandy Wadgers. The stranger shouts that he had done nothing to be treated like that. A fight between Mr Jaffers and the stranger starts. Finally, the stranger submits.

बॉबी जैफर्स का अजनबी को गिरफ्तार करने आना

गाँव का सिपाही Mr Bobby Jaffers (मि बॉबी जैफर्स) अजनबी को गिरफ्तार करने के लिए आया। लोगों ने उसको सराय में हुई घटना के बारे में बताया। मि जैफर्स ने दृढ़ता से कहा कि चाहे उसका सिर हो या न हो, वह उस आदमी को गिरफ्तार करेगा। मि जैफर्स, मि हॉल और मि सैंडी वेजर्स के साथ गए। अजनबी उनको देखकर चिल्लाया कि उसने कोई ऐसा काम नहीं किया है, जिसके लिए उसे गिरफ्तार किया जाए। मि जैफर्स और अजनबी के बीच लड़ाई शुरू हो गई। अंततः अजनबी ने समर्पण कर दिया।

Word Meaning

Repulse – इंकार/पराजय
Furiously – खतरनाक रूप से
Stride – चहलकदमी
Scared – भयभीत
Pique – गुस्सा होना
Plumes – गर्व
Penetrated – भेद देना
Audible – सुनने योग्य
Smashed – तोड़ देना
Twang – नाक से आने वाली आवाज
Subsequently – परिणामस्वरूप
Fiercer – खतरनाक तरीके से
Remittance – भुगतान
Vividly – बहुरंगा
Stamped – पैर पटकना
Anxious – उत्सुक
Metamorphosed – बदलना
Gesture – ईशारा
Shrieked – चीखना
Hobbledehoy – विचित्र
Venturing – उद्यम करना (हिम्मत करना)
Rumour – अफवाह
Outburst – गुस्सा/खीझ
Resplendent – चमकदार
Picturesque – खूबसूरत
Ensigns – झंडा
Savagely – बुरे तरीके से
Fragments – टुकड़े
Pungent – बदबूदार
Tainted – बेकार कर देना
Sheepishly – चुपके से
Deliberated – विचार करना
Grumble – शिकायत करना
Daresay – मान लेना
Annoy – नाराज होना
Clenched – पकड़ना
Staggered – लड़खड़ाना
Anticipation – उम्मीद
Tangible – छुआ जा सकने वाला
Tumbled – गिरने जैसा

Important Questions

Questions based on the Plot of the Chapter

Q 1. What explanation did Mrs Hall demand from the stranger? How did he react?

मिसेज हॉल ने अजनबी से क्या स्पष्टीकरण माँगा? अजनबी ने कैसी प्रतिक्रिया दी?

अजनबी का बिल न देना – मिसेज हॉल द्वारा अजनबी को दी जा रही सेवाएँ समाप्त कर देना – गुस्से में अजनबी का मिसेज हॉल से पूछना कि सेवा बंद क्यों की गई – मिसेज हॉल द्वारा बिल न चुकाने का कारण बताना – मिसेज हॉल द्वारा पूछना कि कैसे उसने कुर्सी के अंदर आत्मा का प्रवेश करा दिया – वह कब और कहाँ आता-जाता है – अजनबी का गुस्सा होकर अपने चेहरे से पट्टी हटाना – बिना सिर का हो जाना – सबको डराकर वहाँ से भगा देना।

Ans. It was the time when the stranger needs to settle the bill but he was unable to do it. In the consequence his services were curtailed by Mrs Hall. The food and all that were being supplied to him by Mrs Hall was stopped by then. He kept on ringing the bell continuously by but Mrs Hall didn't respond to it by her conscience. Finally, when he could not suppress his anger, he came down and asked for the curtailing in his services.

Mrs Hall asked him for the unsettled bills. After that she asked him to explain it first how did he made the chair move in his room. She wanted to let him say his coming and going without being noticed by anybody. When Mrs Hall put up all of the queries that were in her mind.

The stranger got irritated and he started to behave in a very rude manner. He told her that she didn't know him and he would show what he was. Then he started to put off all the bandages from his face and started to get disappeared from the vicinity. This was the most scaring moment and everybody started to run away from there.

Q 2. "You don't understand," he said, "who I am or what I am. I'll show you. By Heaven! I'll show you." What did the stranger show to the crowd gathered at the inn?

अजनबी ने कहा, "तुम्हें पता नहीं है कि मैं कौन हूँ, और क्या हूँ। मैं आज तुम्हें दिखाता हूँ।" उसने भीड़ को क्या दिखाया?

अजनबी द्वारा समय पर बिल न चुकाना – उसकी सेवाओं को मिसेज हॉल द्वारा बंद कर देना – लगातार घंटी बजाना – भूख की वजह से चिल्लाना – गुस्से में उसका नीचे आना और पूछना – मिसेज हॉल का बिल चुकाने को कहना – इसके अलावा उससे कुर्सी के जीवंत होने व उसके आने-जाने के संबंध में पूछना – अजनबी का गुस्सा होना और अपने चेहरे से पट्टी को हटाना – अजनबी का बिना सिर वाला होना – भीड़ का डरकर भागना।

Ans. There was an accumulation of some unpaid bills. It was to be settled by the stranger. But, as he had not enough money left with him so he was unable to settle the dues against his name. This resulted into the curtailing of some or partially all services that were being given to him by Mrs Hall.

He waited and waited and kept on ringing the bell to Mrs Hall for the resumption of the services. But nothing had been taken into account. Hunger was surmounting alongwith withered anger. Finally, the stranger came down and called for Mrs Hall.

When she appeared, he demanded that his services must be resumed. But Mrs Hall rejected the plea by saying that the bills are still to get settled. Moreover she was asking him some sort of explanations like how did the chair become alive and when did he come and go from his room.

When all this was taking place, he thundered everybody by saying that they didn't know who he was and what he was! He started to take off all the bandages from his face and then became headless. That was enough to create panic in the minds of the crowd that was standing there in the inn.

Question based on the Character Sketch

Q 3. "Head or no head," said Jaffers, "I got to arrest him and I will arrest him". Bobby Jaffers was a man of determination and a dutiful man. What impression does he leave on the mind of the reader?

''सिर हो या न हो'' मि जैफर्स ने कहा, ''मैं उसको गिरफ्तार करने आया हूँ और गिरफ्तार करके जाऊँगा।'' मि बॉबी जैफर्स एक दृढ़ प्रतिज्ञ तथा कर्त्तव्यनिष्ठ इंसान थे। आप उनके बारे में क्या राय रखते हैं?

अजनबी द्वारा दहशत फैलाना – मि जैफर्स को बुलाया जाना – लोगों द्वारा बताया जाना कि अजनबी बिना सिर वाला एक इंसान – जैफर्स का निश्चय करना कि वह उसे गिरफ्तार करेगा – जैफर्स का अजनबी के कमरे में जाना – दोनों के बीच लड़ाई शुरू होना – अजनबी का आत्मसमर्पण करना – मि जैफर्स को धोखा देकर अजनबी का गायब होना – अदृश्य होकर जैफर्स को मारकर बेहोश करना – जैफर्स का साबित करना कि उसने हर संभव प्रयास किया कि वह उसे गिरफ्तार कर सके।

Ans. It was the stranger and his grave acts that lead to the calling of the village constable Mr Jaffers. People of Iping were deeply troubled and when they saw no means of getting rid of the situation, Mr Jaffers was called. When Mr Jaffers arrived at the spot, till the time the stranger had created much of hue and cry there. When he reached, he took Mr Hall and Mr Sandy Wedgers alongwith him and he went on ahead with the intention of getting the man arrested.

People told Mr Jaffers that the man had got no head, but Mr Jaffers was not moved with that. He had got an arrest warrant against the stranger and he was determined to let the law take its own course without any interruption. He was dutiful too. So, he didn't care about the man had no head.

He went into the room of the stranger and then both lead into a bitter fight. Suddenly the stranger submitted in front of Mr Jaffers that indicates that he was really determined about what his task was. Then, Mr Jaffers was deceived by the stranger but he didn't give way to him. He fought against him until he was unconscious and the convict made the easy escape.

In Transit

Mr Gibbons' Unusual Experience

Mr Gibbons, a naturalist, was spending his day out in the open fields when he heard someone. He was sure that someone was sneezing and swearing and probably the man was a literate one. But to his astonishment, he could spot no one. Gibbons heard the swearing rise as if the person was near and then the sounds faded away. He was very scared and ran towards the village.

मि गिबंस का अजीबोगरीब अनुभव

Mr Gibbons (मि गिबंस), एक प्रकृति प्रेमी, बाहर खुले मैदानों में अपना दिन व्यतीत कर रहे थे तभी उन्होनें किसी की आवाज सुनी। वे पक्के तौर पर कह सकते थे कि कोई छींक रहा था और बोल रहा था और शायद वह व्यक्ति शिक्षित था। परंतु देखने पर उन्हें वहाँ कोई नहीं मिला। गिबंस को वह आवाज बढ़ती हुई प्रतीत हुई जैसे कि वह व्यक्ति उसके पास आ रहा हो और फिर वह आवाज समाप्त हो गई। गिबंस बहुत डर गया था और गाँव की तरफ भागा।

Word Meaning

- Exceedingly – बहुत
- Naturalist – प्रकृति प्रेमी
- Dozing – ऊँघना
- Indisputable – विवाद से परे
- Cultivated – शिक्षित
- Spasmodic – अनियमित
- Vanished – गायब हो जाना
- Amateur – शौकीन
- Spacious – खुला-खुला
- Beheld – ध्यान से देखना
- Distinguishes – साफ तौर पर
- Climax – चरम
- Tranquility – शांति

Important Questions

Question based on the Plot of the Chapter

Q 1. Whom do you think Mr Gibbons had heard? Give reasons to support your answer.

मि गिबंस ने किसकी आवाज सुनी? अपने उत्तर के समर्थन में कारण दीजिए।

अजनबी का बिना सिर वाला होना – मदद के लिए सिपाही जैफर्स को बुलाना – अजनबी का जैफर्स को चकमा देना – अजनबी का आइपिंग से भाग जाना – उसका खाने के लिए खेतों मे कुछ खोजना – मि गिबंस का उसकी छींके सुनना – उनका विश्वास कि व्यक्ति शिक्षित होना – मि गिबंस का आइपिंग की घटना से अंजान होना – तथ्यों के आधार पर लगना कि अजनबी ने ही मि गिंबस को डराया था।

Ans. The voice that Mr Gibbons would have heard must be of the stranger. We can support the statement. Since morning, whatever was going on, all the way was full of mystery and the element of miracle.

The person became headless and scared the people at the inn. After that the village constable was called and he went into the room of the stranger to get the man arrested. But he was deceived by the stranger and made his escape. Now, the stranger must have been running somewhere out of Iping and he must have had his way to the fields of Iping so that he might get something to eat.

He would have reached the fields where Mr Gibbons would have seated himself and the stranger was heard there. Mr Gibbons had mentioned sneezing and swearing. He had also said that whoever it was, a literate person indeed.

The stranger had been heard even sneezing in the inn by the Halls and there was no doubt that he was a literate man. Moreover, Mr Gibbons was unaware of events that had been going on in Iping and events suggested that the person must be the stranger. Therefore, we can say that the person that Mr Gibbons had heard was surely the man being the stranger.

Mr Thomas Marvel

Mr Thomas Marvel

Mr Thomas Marvel, a naturalist person. He was a short and fat man. He did everything leisurely. When he was sitting near the road, he was pondering over the pair of shoes that he must wear. He had two pairs of shoes and was unable to decide which one would be the best to wear.

Coming of the Voice

While Mr Marvel was lost in his musings about the shoes, a voice came from behind. He was so busy with the shoes that he didn't bother to look at the person. Finally, when Mr Marvel turned, he saw that there was no one behind him. Mr Marvel was very shocked.

Marvel's Confusion

Mr Marvel was confused as he could hear someone talking to him but could not see the person. He thought that someone was trying to fool him. He thought that he was either drunk or having a vision. However, the voice asked him not to be alarmed and to keep his nerves steady.

The Invisible Man

The Invisible Man decided to make Mr Marvel realise that he was indeed real by throwing flints at him. One of them hit poor Mr Marvel. The Invisible Man further told Mr Marvel that he was a human being but only invisible. Mr Marvel was still having a hard time believing it. He asked for the Invisible Man's hand. Mr Marvel touched his hand and realised that it was rather skinny.

Mr Thomas Marvel

मि थॉमस मार्वेल

Mr Thomas Marvel (मि थॉमस मार्वेल), एक प्रकृति प्रेमी व्यक्ति हैं। वह छोटे कद के मोटे व्यक्ति थे। वह सब कुछ आराम से करते थे। जब वह सड़क के किनारे बैठे थे, तो वह अपने जूतों के बारे में सोच रहे थे कि कौन-सा जूता पहना जाए। उनके पास दो जोड़ी जूते थे और वे तय नहीं कर पा रहे थे कि कौन-सा जूता पहनने के लिए सबसे अच्छा रहेगा।

आवाज आना

जब Mr Marvel (मि मार्वेल) जूतों के ख्यालों में खोये हुए थे, तभी पीछे से एक आवाज आई। वे अपने जूतों के ख्याल में इतने व्यस्त थे कि उन्होंने उस व्यक्ति को देखने का कष्ट नहीं किया। अंततः जब मि मार्वेल पीछे मुड़े, तो देखा कि वहाँ पर कोई नहीं था। मि मार्वेल को बहुत आश्चर्य हुआ।

मि मार्वेल की व्याकुलता

मि मार्वेल व्याकुल हो गए, जब उन्होंने खुद से बातें करने वाली आवाज सुनी, परंतु वह किसी को देख नहीं पाए। उन्हें लगा कि कोई उनके साथ मजाक कर रहा है। उन्होंने सोचा या तो यह शराब का नशा है या वह सपना देख रहे हैं। हालाँकि, आवाज ने उन्हें न चौंकने और अपने दिमाग को शांत रखने के लिए कहा।

अदृश्य आदमी

अदृश्य आदमी ने निश्चय किया कि वह मि मार्वेल को उनके ऊपर पत्थर फेंककर अपने जीवंत होने का अहसास कराएगा। एक पत्थर मि मार्वेल को जाकर लगा। अदृश्य आदमी ने मि मार्वेल को बताया कि वह भी एक सामान्य इंसान है लेकिन वह केवल अदृश्य है। मि मार्वेल को इस पर विश्वास करने में बहुत समय लगा। उन्होंने अदृश्य आदमी से उसके हाथ के लिए कहा। मि मार्वेल ने उसके हाथ को छुआ और खाल को महसूस किया।

The Invisible Man Asks for Help

The Invisible Man informed Mr Marvel that being invisible was no easy business and he wanted some help. Mr Marvel was confused. He didn't know how he could be of any help to the man. The Invisible Man said that he would be of great help to him. The Invisible Man threatened him that if Mr Marvel betrayed him, the consequences would be severe. Mr Marvel had no choice but to submit.

अदृश्य आदमी का मदद माँगना

अदृश्य आदमी ने मि मार्वेल को बताया कि गायब होना कोई आसान काम नहीं है और उसे किसी की मदद की जरूरत है। मि मार्वेल दुविधा में पड़ गए। वे नहीं जानते थे कि वे अदृश्य आदमी की कोई मदद कैसे कर सकता है। अदृश्य आदमी ने कहा कि वह उसके लिए बहुत सहायक हो सकता है। अदृश्य आदमी ने कहा कि यदि मि मार्वेल ने उसे धोखा देने की कोशिश की, तो उसका परिणाम बहुत गंभीर होगा। मि मार्वेल के पास समर्पण करने के अलावा कोई और विकल्प नहीं था।

Word Meaning

Copious - बड़ा
Visage - चेहरा
Protrusion - चीजें जो बाहर आती हैं
Ample - प्रचुर मात्रा में
Peewit - एक प्रकार की चिड़िया
Irradiated - खुश करना
Shuffling - आगे-पीछे करना
Chump - मूर्ख
Flints - पत्थर के टुकड़े
Rapidity - जल्दबाजी
Ricochetted - सीधा और तेज चलना
Obstacle - बाधा
Jabber - बेकार बोलने वाला
Timorously - डरते हुए
Astonishment - आश्चर्य होना
Scrutinised - जाँच-पड़ताल करना
Contemplating - सोच-विचार करना
Flexible - लचीला
Cylindrical - सुराहीदार
Liquorish - जिसे शराब पसंद हो
Fluctuating - लगातार बदलना
Rage - गुस्सा
Desolate - सुनसान
Blarsted - विस्फोट होना
Tremulous - काँपता हुआ
Complicated - उलझन भरा
Dodge - त्यागना
Howled - चिल्लाना
Confounded - हैरान
Disengaged - अलग करना
Patted - थपथपाना
Dashed - भाग जाना
Assimilated - सटीक बनाना
Modest - सरल व साधारण

Important Questions

Questions based on the Plot of the Chapter

Q 1. Who was Mr Marvel? What was he doing when the voice interrupted him?

मि मार्वेल कौन थे? जब आवाज ने उन्हें बाधित किया, तो वे क्या कर रहे थे?

मि मार्वेल आइपिंग के निवासी – उनका प्रकृति प्रेमी और खुले दिल वाले इंसान होना – अपना काम शांति से करने की इच्छा – आस-पास की घटनाओं से प्रभावित न होना – शराब पीना पसंद करना – एक दिन घर से दूर बैठे होना – दो जोड़ी जूतों में से यह निश्चित करना कि कौन-सा पहना जाए – पीछे से एक आवाज आना – दोनों का जूतों के ऊपर चर्चा करना – मि मार्वेल का पीछे मुड़कर देखना – वहाँ कोई आदमी न होना – मि मार्वेल को लगना कि किसी ने मजाक किया है – उनको लगना कि शायद शराब पीने के कारण ऐसा हो रहा है।

Ans. Mr Marvel was a resident of Iping. He loved nature very much. He was a carefree man and always loved to do his business in a way that was leisurely. He never minded to be bothered by the happening around him.

As his nature was, he was very much of likes of liquorish and he often consumed liquor. One day, when he walked out from his home a mile and half and seated himself near a ditch, he had got two pairs of shoes with him. He wanted to pick one of the pairs but was in a dilemma, which one to choose.

He could not decide it and was busy at his own musings over the shoes. Suddenly, he heard a sound from the backside and the sound too, was falling in a row with the shoes. There came suggestions and all that.

Both went on with their conversation, but when Mr Marvel intended to look back his interlocutor, he found none there. This was his surprise that with whom he was talking to if he could not see anyone back.

Marvel took it to be someone who was playing a prank with him and thinking that the man was trying to fool him. Another thought was that his drink had got better of him then.

Q 2. What did the Invisible Man do to show Mr Marvel that he was no imagination?

अजनबी ने मि मार्वेल को यकीन दिलाने हेतु, कि वह कोई कल्पना नहीं है, क्या किया?

अजनबी का आइपिंग छोड़ने पर भोजन, कपड़े इत्यादि के लिए इधर-उधर भटकना – मार्वेल का अपने दो जोड़ी जूते लेकर परेशान होना – अजनबी की मि मार्वेल से मुलाकात और बातचीत होना – मार्वेल का अपने साथी को देखने के लिए पीछे मुड़ना – साथी का वहाँ पर न होना – आवाज लगातार सुनाई देना – अजनबी का कहना कि वह अदृश्य है – मार्वेल को यकीन न होना – अजनबी का उस पर पत्थर मारना व अपना हाथ आगे देना – मार्वेल को यकीन हो जाना।

Ans. When the invisible man was wandering out in the open and far-flung area of Iping, he was actually hoping a helping hand for himself who can help him with food, clothes and all that.

He met Mr Marvel by chance who was sitting beside a ditch with two pairs of shoes and trying to decide which one he should wear. The invisible man started a conversation with Mr Marvel thinking that he might be a man of help.

He started the discussion with shoes and as Mr Marvel tried to locate who was talking with him, he found none to his great surprise.

He was shocked when the sound was coming without any physical source involved. Then, he heard the same sound saying that he was an invisible man.

It took so long for Mr Marvel to believe the words. Mr Marvel asked for the justification when the man said that he was a human being like him but could not be seen, then stranger gave his hand to Marvel to realise the truth.

He started to throw some stones over the face and the shoulder of Mr Marvel. Then, Mr Marvel believed that he was really invisible. Mr Marvel put his hands around the stranger further to assure his existence.

Q 3. Do you think Mr Marvel willingly submitted to the Invisible Man's demands? Give reasons for your answer.

क्या मि मार्वेल ने अपनी इच्छा से अदृश्य आदमी की माँग पूरी की? अपने उत्तर के समर्थन में कारण दीजिए।

अजनबी और मार्वेल की मुलाकात होना – दोनों के बीच में जूतों के विषय में बातचीत होना – मार्वेल का अजनबी को देखने के लिए पीछे मुड़ना – वहाँ पर किसी का दिखाई न देना – आवाजों का लगातार आना – अजनबी का कहना कि वह अदृश्य है – मि मार्वेल का साक्ष्यों के आधार पर यकीन करना – अजनबी का कहना कि अपनी शक्तियों से वह उसे लाभ देगा – उसे उसकी मदद करनी होगी – अगर मार्वेल इंकार करे, तो उसे बुरे परिणाम मिलेंगे – डर व अनिच्छा से मार्वेल का तैयार होना।

Ans. The stranger and Mr Marvel met by chance when the former was wandering out in Iping and the latter was sitting near ditch. They fell in a conversation related to their shoes.

When the discussion was over, Mr Marvel tried to see his friend who was in the conversation. When Marvel turned back, he located none as a consequence, he was frightened and surprised.

Then the stranger told Marvel that he was a human being just like him and the fact was that he couldn't be seen as he was invisible.

Marvel didn't believe the idea and revoked, but when stones were thrown and the hand was touched, he got to believe the words of the stranger.

The stranger insisted Marvel to be his helper and he would do a lot of goods to him if he did like the way that the stranger wanted. He told Marvel that he had got magical powers and it would be a benefit to him.

If Marvel refuses to do the way he wanted, he must be ready to face the consequences. This frightened Marvel and he submitted then on the threatening of the stranger and not by his own inclination.

Mr Marvel's Visit to Iping

Life Tries to Return to Normalcy in Iping

After the incident of the Invisible Man, life of the Iping folk tried to return to normalcy. However, there were still doubts in the minds of the people. However, the witnesses Mr Sandy Wedgers and Mr Jaffers could not come out of their trauma in utter shock.

The Second Stranger Enters Iping

While the people were engrossed in festivities, second stranger entered the village. The people of Iping could recognise that he was actually Mr Marvel by his appearance and the sort of clothes that he was wearing.

The Stranger Enters the Inn

Initially, the stranger was not ready to enter the 'Coach and Horses', but then took his time to make up his mind and entered. There he saw Mrs Hall. All this time, Mr Huxter was keeping a keen eye on him.

Mr Huxter's Chase is Brought

Mr Huxter's suspicion was right. The stranger was a thief. He had stolen some books. Mr Huxter ran to catch him. Mr Huxter began chasing him yelling 'thief'. But before he could catch the man, something tripped Mr Huxter and knocked him out. He saw the ground suddenly close to his face.

Mr Marvel's Visit to Iping

आइपिंग में जीवन सामान्य होना

अदृश्य आदमी की घटना के बाद, आइपिंग में जीवन धीरे-धीरे सामान्य होने लगा था। हालाँकि, इसके बाद भी लोगों के दिमाग में शक था। हालाँकि, Mr Sandy Wedgers (मि सैंडी वेजर्स) और Mr Jaffers (मि जैफर्स), जो उस घटना के प्रत्यक्षदर्शी थे, उस सदमे से बाहर नहीं आ पाए थे।

दूसरे अजनबी का आइपिंग में प्रवेश

जब व्यक्ति उत्सव की तैयारी में लगे हुए थे तभी दूसरे अजनबी ने गाँव में प्रवेश किया। आइपिंग के लोग उसके दिखावे और कपड़े जो उसने पहने हुए थे, देखकर पहचान सकते थे कि वह वास्तव मे Mr Marvel (मि मार्वेल) है।

अजनबी का सराय में प्रवेश करना

शुरूआत में अजनबी 'Coach and Horses' ('कोच एण्ड हॉर्सेज') के अंदर जाने के लिए तैयार नहीं था, परंतु कुछ समय के बाद उसने मन बनाया और अंदर चला गया। उसने वहाँ मिसेज हॉल को देखा। पूरे समय Mr Huxter (मि हक्सटर) ने उस पर नजर जमाए रखी।

मि हक्सटर का पीछा करना

मि हक्सटर का शक सही था। अजनबी एक चोर था। उसने कुछ किताबें चुराई थीं। मि हक्सटर उसे पकड़ने के लिए उसके पीछे भागे। मि हक्सटर उसका पीछा करने लगे और 'चोर-चोर' चिल्लाने लगे। लेकिन इससे पहले कि वह उसे पकड़ पाते, किसी वस्तु ने मि हक्सटर को उलझाया और उन्हें गिरा दिया। वह मैदान में औंधे मुँह गिर गए।

Word Meaning

Gusty Panic – भयंकर लड़ाई
Skepticism – शक करने वाला
Stunned – आश्चर्यचकित
Tangible – वास्तविक
Gala dress – उत्सव के कपड़े
Tentative – अस्त-व्यस्त
Curate – निगरानी करने वाला
Qualms – शक
Hurled – जोर से चिल्लाना
Promenading – टहलना
Splendid – शानदार
Delicately – बारीकी से
Mottled – निश्चित करना
Furtive – गुप्त रूप से
Languid – आलसी
Prompted – जल्दीबाजी
Conceiving – कल्पना करना
Intercept – रोकना
Braces – बाँधना
Inadvertently – गैर-इरादतन
Induce – उत्साहित करना
Whirling – घूमते हुए
Spurting – तेजी से निकल जाना
Curses – शाप देना
Athwart – के खिलाफ
Multitude – बहुत ज्यादा
Reluctantly – अनिच्छा से
Crepitation – घर्षण
Witch Craft – काला जादू
Apprentice – नवसिखुआ
Accord – इच्छा
Viciously – बुरे तरीके से
Terminated – समाप्ति होना
Inclined – इरादतन
Accentuated – साफ-साफ दिखना
Pricked – चुभना
Turf – सतह
Argumentative – झगड़ालू
Impregnably – जिसे पकड़ा न जा सके
Transcending – बीतता हुआ
Bunting – सजावट
Amusements – मनोरंजन
Jest – खुशी
Conceal – छिपाना
Clinging – चिपक जाना
Adolescents – प्रौढ़ावस्था
Pungent – बदबूदार
Adorned – सजाया जाना
Apprehensive – अवधारणा होना
Alacrity – उतावलापन
Clumsily – भद्दा तरीका
Belied – छिपा हुआ
Vanished – गायब होना
Larceny – चोरी
Askew – तिरछा करना
Peculiar – विचित्र
Perceptions – समझ
Apprising – प्रचार-प्रसार करना
Specks – बिंदु
Mumbled – फुसफुसाना
Resolute – दृढ़-प्रतिज्ञा
Raving – जंगली
Hobnails – छोटी कीलें
Soliloquy – खुद से बातचीत करना
Customary – परंपरागत
Gentry – उच्च वर्गीय लोग
Asserted – बरकरार रखना
Amazement – आश्चर्य
Tremendous – बहुत ज्यादा
Bristling – सख्त बाल
Embonpoint – शरीर का मांसल हिस्सा
Ditch – गड्ढा
Damp – नमी
Agrimony – एक प्रकार का पौधा

Important Questions

Questions based on the Plot of the Chapter

Q 1. Great and strange ideas transcending experience often have less effect upon men and women than smaller, more tangible considerations. Comment.

इंसानों पर कभी-कभी बड़ी चीजों का इतना असर नहीं होता जितना कि छोटी-छोटी चीजों का होता है। पाठ के संदर्भ में व्याख्या करें।

इंसानी स्वभाव का परिवर्तनशील होना – हमारा कई बार घटनाओं से सीख न लेना – बाद में इसका एक बड़ा नुकसान बन जाना – आइपिंग निवासियों का इसी अनुभव से गुजरना – उनका अजनबी के असमय आने की घटना को नहीं समझ पाना – मिसेज हॉल की व्यापारिक लाभ की चाहत का बलवती हो जाना – एक बड़े मुद्दे का धीरे-धीरे नजरअंदाज होना – लोगों का इससे अनुभव न लेना – कथन का सही होना कि लोग बड़ी चीजों से अक्सर नहीं सीख पाते।

Ans. Human nature is all the way unpredictable and unprecedented. No one is certain with ideas and taste. It does change often with a change in the circumstances.

We often miss a lesson that an incident can give us and later on it proves to be a loss that is beyond compensation. But, this is what life is all about and that is how life goes on.

It does happen often when we can't take the due lesson from the great and strange ideas, but we are a bit more keen to take the lesson from the smaller one. Villagers at Iping had gone through the same kind of experience.

Yet, they were sophisticated and civilised, but they were not able to take the note from it. They must be in action when the unusual arrival of the stranger took place in Iping, but they were not.

Specially, Mrs Hall was eager to have a good unseasonal business but she didn't pay any heed towards it. It became a big issue with the passage of time and it was more difficult to handle the case later on.

That is the big and great situation to gain the hint, but what happened was beyond the thinking of the folks. So, it could well be said that we often miss the lesson from great and strange experience in our lives.

Q 2. How was Mr Huxter's Chase brought to a halt? Who do you think was responsible for it?

मि हक्सटर का पीछा करना कैसे रुक गया? इसके लिए कौन जिम्मेदार हो सकता है?

आइपिंग छोड़ने के बाद अजनबी का एक सहायक दोस्त की तलाश करना – उसकी मुलाकात मि मार्वेल से होना – अजनबी द्वारा मि मार्वेल को जबरदस्ती अपना काम कराने को तैयार करना – मि मार्वेल का अनिच्छा से तैयार हो जाना – मि मार्वेल का धर्मशाला की तरफ आना – मि हक्सटर को मि मार्वेल पर शक होना – किताबें चुराकर मि मार्वेल का बाहर आना – हक्सटर द्वारा मि मार्वेल का पीछा करना – रास्ते में अचानक मि हक्सटर का गिर जाना व पीछा करना छोड़ देना – घटना के पीछे अदृश्य आदमी का हाथ होना – उसके ही द्वारा हक्सटर को गिराना, ताकि मि मार्वेल किताबें लेकर भाग सकें।

Ans. The Invisible Man went out of Iping in the search of a person who could be a friend of him and could give him a helping hand as he was in a desperate need of it.

The stranger met Mr Marvel on the down side and had a conversation with him. In the end, the stranger revealed himself as a man who could not be seen and he threatened Mr Marvel that had he refused to help him then he must be ready for the direst things. If Mr Marvel offers his help to stranger, he would benefit him with magical powers. Then, Mr Marvel agreed and went to the inn to bring the books of the stranger.

Mr Huxter was having a keen eye on the new stranger. He saw that Mr Marvel was reluctant to go there and after sometime he went inside. Mr Marvel came out of the inn with the books in his hand. Mr Huxter's doubt was confirmed and he gave a chase to Mr Marvel. As Mr Marvel was running and Mr Huxter was behind him, strangely Mr Huxter had hit upon his shin and then he fell down and abruptly gave-up the chase. One must say the falling of Mr Huxter was due to the strange man who would have hit him. He was standing there invisible and that had allowed Mr Marvel to escape with his important books with him.

Question based on the Character Sketch

Q 3. Mr Huxter was a keen observer and he instantly guessed the reason for the strange man's behaviour. In the light of this statement, attempt a character sketch of Mr Huxter.

मि हक्सटर एक अच्छे जागरुक प्रेक्षक थे और उन्होंने अजनबी के व्यवहार को तुरंत देख लिया था। इस कथन के परिप्रेक्ष्य में उनका चरित्र चित्रण करें।

अदृश्य आदमी की मदद के लिए मि मार्वेल का जबर्दस्ती तैयार होना – अजीबोगरीब तरीके से उसे धमकाना – मि मार्वेल का अदृश्य आदमी की किताबें चुराने के लिए धर्मशाला जाना – धर्मशाला के बाहर जाने पर मि मार्वेल का हक्सटर की नजरों में आ जाना – मि हक्सटर का उस पर शक करना और लगातार नजर बनाए रखना – मि मार्वेल का चोरी करने के बाद बाहर आना – मि हक्सटर का पीछा करना – तब तक पीछा करना जब तक वह गिर न गए – मि हक्सटर की जागरूकता का प्रमाण होना।

Ans. When Mr Marvel was forced by the Invisible Man to be his helper, it was the start of a new phase of Mr Marvel's life. He was severely threatened of the direst results if he didn't help the Invisible Man. Forced and obliged by the circumstances, he had to do as per the wish of the Invisible Man.

To start with, the Invisible Man forced him to make a thievery at the inn for his own books. Mr Marvel was waiting outside the inn when Mr Huxter saw him for the first time and started to ponder if this man had anything to do with Iping. He got the impression that Mr Marvel had never been seen here in Iping and thus another strange man was at the inn.

He kept on having a close look at the inn and at the movement of the strange man. When Mr Marvel entered the inn, he was still under the keen eyes of Mr Huxter. As the thievery took place, Mr Huxter noticed that and started to give a chase. He was severely hit by something out of nowhere and fell down.

Till then, he gave Mr Marvel a pulsating chase. This shows that Mr Huxter had the sense of realising the wrong ones that are going on in his surroundings and he could not submit to these so easily.

In the "Coach and Horses"

Mr Cuss and Mr Bunting are in the Invisible Man's Room

The narrator takes the reader into flashback to explain the events that happened when Mr Marvel had made his first visit to Iping. Mr Cuss and Mr Bunting were in the Invisible Man's room. Mrs Hall had given them permission to examine the Invisible Man's belongings.

The Invisible Man's Diaries

Mr Cuss found the three diaries that belonged to the Invisible Man. Mr Cuss was happy as now he hoped for getting some clues about the Invisible Man. But the diaries were written in some sort of code. The two were unable to make out what it said. Mr Cuss thought that perhaps it was in Greek and Mr Bunting could read it. Unfortunately, Mr Bunting had forgotten all his Greek.

Mr Marvel Intrudes in the Room

Just then, the two investigators were interrupted by Mr Marvel. They thought that perhaps it was a sailor. In fact, Mr Marvel had led the Invisible Man in. Mr Bunting argued that he did not believe in the story of the Invisible Man. He thought that perhaps what the people saw was a work of some magician.

In the "Coach and Horses"

मि कस व मि बंटिंग का अदृश्य आदमी के कमरे में जाना

The Narrator (वर्णनकर्ता) पाठक को उस घटना की व्याख्या करने के लिए पूर्वदृश्य में ले जाता है, जब Mr Marvel (मि मार्वेल) पहली बार Iping (आइपिंग) आए थे। Mr Cuss and Mr Bunting (मि कस और मि बंटिंग) अदृश्य आदमी के कमरे में थे। Mrs Hall (मिसेज हॉल) ने उनको अदृश्य आदमी के सामान की जाँच-पड़ताल करने की अनुमति प्रदान की।

अदृश्य आदमी की डायरियाँ

मि कस को अदृश्य आदमी से संबंधित तीन डायरियाँ मिल गईं। मि कस खुश थे कि शायद उन्हें अब अदृश्य आदमी के बारे में कुछ जानकारी मिल जाएगी। परंतु डायरियाँ एक तरह की कोड भाषा में लिखी हुई थीं। दोनों को यह समझ नहीं आया कि इनमें क्या लिखा है। मि कस को लगा कि डायरी Greek (ग्रीक) भाषा में लिखी हैं और मि बंटिंग शायद इसे पढ़ सकें। दुर्भाग्यवश, मि बंटिंग सारी ग्रीक भाषा भूल गए थे।

मि मार्वेल का यकायक कमरे में आना

जब दोनों अंदर जाँच-पड़ताल कर रहे थे, तभी मि मार्वेल भी आ गए। उन्होंने सोचा कि शायद यह कोई नाविक है। वास्तव में, मि मार्वेल अदृश्य आदमी को वहाँ पर लेकर आए थे। मि बंटिंग ने कहा कि वे अदृश्य आदमी से जुड़ी कहानी पर यकीन नहीं करते हैं। उनका मानना था कि शायद जो कुछ भी लोगों ने देखा वह किसी जादूगर का काम था।

Word Meaning

Wont	– आदत होना	Cypher	– कूट भाषा
Fastidiously	– सावधानी से	Avert	– बचने की कोशिश करना
Inevitable	– जिसे छोड़ा न जा सके	Sporadically	– पता लग जाना
Huskiness	– खुरदरापन	Nautical	– समुद्री
Indisputable	– विवाद से परे	Absurd	– संवेदनाहीन
Hallucinations	– छलावा	Conjuror	– जादूगर
Thrashed	– पटका मारना	Flushed	– चमक उठना
Nape	– कॉलर	Pry into	– जाँचना
Memoranda	– लिखी गई बातें	Rattled	– गिरा देना
Invade	– घुसपैठ	Concussion	– कथन
Wriggling	– झटका मारना	Stark	– नंगा
Mumbled	– फुसफुसाना	Curses	– शाप देना
Resolute	– दृढ़-प्रतिज्ञा	Athwart	– के खिलाफ
Raving	– जंगली	Multitude	– बहुत ज्यादा
Hobnails	– छोटी कीलें	Reluctantly	– अनिच्छा से
Soliloquy	– खुद से बातचीत करना	Crepitation	– घर्षण
Customary	– परंपरागत	Witch Craft	– काला जादू
Gentry	– उच्च वर्गीय लोग	Apprentice	– नवसिखुआ
Asserted	– बरकरार रखना	Accord	– इच्छा
Amazement	– आश्चर्य	Viciously	– बुरे तरीके से

Important Questions

Question based on the Plot of the Chapter

Q 1. Why were the two investigators left disappointed even after they got their hands on the Invisible Man's diaries?

दोनों जाँचकर्ताओं को अदृश्य आदमी की निजी डायरी के मिलने के बाद भी निराशा क्यों हाथ लगी?

मि कस और मि बंटिंग का अजनबी के कमरे में मिसेज हॉल की आज्ञा से जाना – दोनों को अजनबी की तीन डायरियाँ मिल जाना – दोनों का एक-दूसरे को कहना कि किसी भी हाल में उन्हें अजनबी के बारे में जानकरी लेनी होगी – डायरियों को खोलने के बाद मि कस को सांकेतिक भाषा में कुछ लिखा हुआ मिलना – मि कस का अनुमान कि यह ग्रीक भाषा है – मि कस का मि बंटिंग को डायरियाँ देना – मि बंटिंग का ग्रीक बहुत पहले भूल जाना – दोनों को डायरियाँ हाथ लगने के बाद भी कुछ जानकारी न मिल पाना।

Ans. As Iping was about to settle after the mess created by the stranger, Mr Cuss and Mr Bunting, most curious men in Iping, came up with the idea of investigating the room of the stranger. They were armed with permission of Mrs Hall and entered the room of the stranger. When they entered the room they found three diaries lying near the table.

They quoted to each other that this was the chance and they must understand something about the strange man at any cost. They started to poke their noses into the diaries they had.

At first, they got to know that these diaries are basically coded and didn't contain any information worth to them. But, Mr Cuss predicted that the code is not the exact code but it was Greek and he knew that Mr Bunting had some idea about the Greek.

Question based on the Character Sketch

Q 2. "For he had no Greek left in his mind worth talking about;" Mr Bunting pretended that he knew Greek when he had forgotten it completely. In light of the statement, attempt a character sketch of Mr Bunting.

''अब उन्हें ग्रीक कुछ तीक ढंग से नहीं याद थी''। मि बंटिंग ने ग्रीक भूल जाने के बाद भी कहा कि शायद वह कुछ जानकारी हासिल कर सकें। इस कथन का संदर्भ लेते हुए उनका चरित्र चित्रण करें।

मि बंटिंग चर्च के पादरी – एक बुद्धिमान व समझदार इंसान – उनका धैर्यपूर्वक दूसरों की बातें सुनना – उनके घर चोरी होने पर भी उनका न घबराना – डंडा लेकर साहस के साथ उसका सामना करना – उनका बहादुर और हार न मानने वाले होना – अपनी जानकारी पर्याप्त न होने पर भी उस पर भरोसा करना – कभी-कभी दिखावा भी करना – कुल मिलाकर सिद्धांतवादी व सुलझे हुए इंसान होना।

Ans. Mr Bunting was the vicar at the local church and he was a rational man. He was reputed for his wisdom and rationality. It was the time when Mr Bunting came to the scene. He was first contacted by Mr Cuss when he had his own experience with the stranger. Mr Bunting heard his story very patiently. This reflects the aspect of his very character that is his patience. Next, his own house was robbed by the stranger in the dawn one day. Even at this time vicar had his courage and he picked up a poker so that he could fight with the robber. This shows that he was brave and courageous. He was a man who would not give-up so easily.

The Invisible Man Loses his temper

Curious Sounds from the Parlour

Mr Teddy and Mr Hall heard some curious sounds coming from the Invisible Man's room. They inquired if the two investigators were all right. They replied not to interrupt them. Things were quite unusual.

Mr Huxter Raises an Alarm

Mrs Hall reprimanded her husband for wasting time on a busy day. Mr Hall did not know of the sounds coming from the parlour. Mr Hall thought that probably the two investigators were engrossed in their work. Just then Mr Huxter raised an alarm.

Everybody Started Chasing Mr Marvel

After Mr Huxter, the crowd started to chase Mr Marvel. Everybody thought that Mr Marvel was the Invisible Man, who had suddenly become visible. The men in pursuit were then attacked by the Invisible Man.

The Invisible Man Lost His Temper

Everybody was running helter-skelter and whosoever came in the Invisible Man's way was hurt. Initially, he just wanted to help Mr Marvel escape, but then he lost his temper and started hurting people just for satisfaction. He even broke every single window of the 'Coach and Horses'. The incident left the village of Iping as if in ruins.

The Invisible Man Loses his temper

बैठक से विचित्र आवाजें आना

Mr Teddy (मि टेडी) और Mr Hall (मि हॉल) ने अदृश्य आदमी के कमरे से कुछ Curious Sounds (विचित्र आवाजें) आती सुनीं। उन्होंने यह पता करने की कोशिश की कि क्या वे दोनों जाँचकर्ता ठीक थे। अंदर से उन दोनों ने कहा कि उन्हें बाधित न किया जाए। अजीब-सी स्थिति बन पड़ी थी।

मि हक्सटर ने शोर मचाया

Mrs Hall (मिसेज हॉल) ने अपने पति का समय खराब करने के लिए खूब खिंचाई की। मि हॉल को बैठक से आ रही आवाजों के बारे में कुछ नहीं पता था। मि हॉल ने सोचा कि दोनों शोधकर्ता अपने काम में व्यस्त हैं। तभी Mr Huxter (मि हक्सटर) ने शोर मचाना शुरू कर दिया।

भीड़ के द्वारा मि मार्वेल का पीछा

मि हक्सटर के बाद, भीड़ ने Mr Marvel (मि मार्वेल) का पीछा करना शुरू कर दिया। सभी ने यह सोचा कि मि मार्वेल ही अदृश्य इंसान है, जो अचानक दृश्य हो गया है। इसके बाद अदृश्य इंसान ने पूरी भीड़ पर हमला कर दिया।

अदृश्य आदमी का गुस्सा आसमान पर

प्रत्येक इंसान इधर-उधर भाग रहा था और जो कोई भी उस अदृश्य आदमी के रास्ते में आया उसे उसने चोट पहुचाँई। प्रारंभ में अदृश्य आदमी मि मार्वेल की भागने में मदद करना चाहता था, परंतु गुस्सा आने के बाद उसने लोगों को भी पीटना शुरू कर दिया। 'Coach and Horses' ('कोच एण्ड हॉर्सेज') में जितनी खिड़कियाँ थीं सबको उसने एक-एक करके तोड़ दिया। इस पूरी घटना ने Iping (आइपिंग) गाँव को खंडहर बना दिया।

Word Meaning

Whiffs	– खुशबू	Intonation	– स्वर शैली
Perplexing	– उधेड़बुन की स्थिति में होना	Grimaces	– चेहरे के हाव-भाव
Obdurate	– जिद्दी	Crestfallen	– निराश होना
Obliquely	– तिरछा	Oblong	– अधिक लंबाई वाला
Incoherent	– तर्कसंगत न होना	Burly	– मज़बूत कद-काठी का
Sprawling	– लेटा हुआ	Absurdly	– बेवकूफी भरा
Kilt	– पहनावा	Bawled	– चिल्लाना
Prostrate	– चिपटा	Indecorous	– असभ्य
Trod	– इधर-उधर घूमना	Rout	– पराजित करना
Startled	– अचंभित होना	Disintegration	– अलगाव होना
Appalled	– डरावनी	Gauds	– एक सजावटी चीज़
Mumbled	– फुसफुसाना	Curses	– शाप देना
Resolute	– दृढ़-प्रतिज्ञा	Athwart	– के खिलाफ
Raving	– जंगली	Multitude	– बहुत ज्यादा
Hobnails	– छोटी कीलें	Reluctantly	– अनिच्छा से
Soliloquy	– खुद से बातचीत करना	Crepitation	– घर्षण

Important Questions

Questions based on the Plot of the Chapter

Q 1. Mr Teddy and Mr Hall heard some curious sounds coming from the Invisible Man's earlier lodgings. What was happening in the room?

मि टेडी और मि हॉल ने अजनबी के कमरे से आने वाली कुछ विचित्र आवाजें सुनीं। कमरे में क्या हो रहा था?

अजनबी के धर्मशाला से बाहर जाने पर लोगों का उसके बारे में जानने के लिए उत्सुक होना – मि बंटिंग व मि कस का उसके कमरे में जाना – वहाँ उन्हें तीन डायरियाँ मिलना – डायरियों का ग्रीक भाषा में लिखा होना – उसके बारे में कोई जानकारी मिलना – इस बीच में मि मार्वेल व अजनबी का कमरे में प्रवेश करना – अपनी डायरियों के साथ देखकर उसका उन दोनों को पीटना और धमकाना

Ans. When the Invisible Man was out of the inn, the curiosity of the folks in Iping was at the peak. To sustain this curiosity, it was decided that Mr Cuss and Mr Bunting would go to the lodgings of the Invisible Man and try to find out whatever information come from there. Therefore, Mr Cuss and Bunting went inside the lodgings of the stranger. When they entered the room of the strange man, they happened to see three diaries that belonged to the Invisible Man and both of the men started to decipher the facts that were written in the diaries. Yet, the diaries were written in Greek and none of the two was so good at Greek even then they were in search of some sort of information from it. In the meantime, both were disturbed by Mr Marvel whom they took to be a sailor and after that, the Invisible Man entered the room and when he saw the two busy with his diaries, he got furious and he thrashed the heads of both the men on the table. After that, the Invisible Man threatened the two that both would be murdered.

Q 2. The men in pursuit of Mr Marvel were routed by an invisible force. Elaborate.

जो लोग मि मार्वेल का पीछा कर रहे थे, उन्हें किसी अदृश्य शक्ति द्वारा रोक लिया गया था। विस्तार से वर्णन करें।

मि बंटिंग व मि कस का अजनबी के कमरे से जानकारी हासिल करना – मि टेडी, मि हॉल और मि हक्सटर का कमरे के बाहर आ जाना – वहाँ हक्सटर का मार्वेल को देखना – हक्सटर के द्वारा शोर मचाने पर लोग उसके पीछे भागे – मि मार्वेल की मदद के लिए अदृश्य आदमी का आगे आना – मार्वेल का पीछा करने वालों पर अदृश्य आदमी द्वारा हमला कर देना – सबको मार-पीटकर घायल कर देना – मार्वेल का आसानी से बचकर निकल जाना।

Ans. When Mr Bunting and Mr Cuss were in the room of the strange man busy with their fest of collecting information about the stranger, at that moment Mr Teddy, Mr Hall and Mr Huxter were standing near the bar that was in front of the inn. As they were near the inn, suddenly Mr Huxter saw Mr Marvel whom he had given a chase earlier too and he raised an alarm. The whole crowd near the inn started to chase Mr Marvel on the command and prompt of Mr Huxter. Marvel was chased by the big folk crowd and that event was seen by the Invisible Man and he was supposed to save his new friend.He used his power that he had got by being invisible and started routing the crowd by coming in between the crowd. He thrashed all the people who ever tried to come in between.

Mr Marvel Discusses His Resignation

The Invisible Man Threatens Mr Marvel

The Invisible Man and Mr Marvel both has left the village of Iping and are walking in the woods. The Invisible Man is very angry with Mr Marvel as the latter tried to run away with his things. Moreover, he is furious that his secret is out now and the incident in Iping would be in the newspapers. He further threatens Mr Marvel of dire consequences if he ever tried to run away again. Mr Marvel denies the accusation.

Mr Marvel Wanted to Resign

Mr Marvel was hopeless. He knew that he was stuck with the Invisible Man. He tried to make him realise that he was not of any use and would probably spoil his plans one day. The Invisible Man kept bullying him. Mr Marvel further tried to convince the Invisible Man that he was too weak to carry out his plans and that he was more of a burden.

Mr Marvel was not Excused

Mr Marvel said that he was too timid and the things wanted of him were devilish hard. He wanted to show the Invisible Man that he was bound to fail. But the Invisible Man was not ready to let him go away.

Mr Marvel had fear in his heart and he wondered what the Invisible Man would ask him to do next.

Mr Marvel Discusses His Resignation

अदृश्य आदमी ने मि मार्वेल को धमकाया

अदृश्य आदमी तथा मि मार्वेल दोनों आइपिंग से निकल चुके थे और जंगल में घूम रहे थे। अदृश्य आदमी मि मार्वेल से बहुत नाराज था क्योंकि मि मार्वेल ने उसकी चीजों को लेकर भागने की कोशिश की थी। इससे भी ज्यादा, अदृश्य आदमी को लग रहा था कि उसके राज़ आइपिंग में खुल चुके हैं और आने वाले समय में यह बात अखबार में आ जाएगी। उसने मि मार्वेल को एक बार फिर धमकाया कि अगर उसने आगे ऐसी कोशिश की तो परिणाम बहुत बुरा होगा। मि मार्वेल ने कहा कि उसने कभी भी यह अपराध नहीं किया है।

मि मार्वेल पद त्यागना चाहते थे

मि मार्वेल बिल्कुल निराश और हताश थे। उन्हें पता था कि वह अदृश्य आदमी के साथ फँस चुके हैं। उन्होनें अदृश्य आदमी को यह अहसास दिलाने की कोशिश की कि वह किसी काम का नहीं है और एक दिन उसकी सारी योजनाओं को चौपट कर देगा। अदृश्य आदमी फिर भी उसे धमकाता रहा। मि मार्वेल ने तब भी अदृश्य आदमी का समझाने की कोशिश की कि वह उसकी योजनाओं के लिए बहुत कमज़ोर है, उसके लिए एक बोझ बन जाएगा।

मि मार्वेल को माफी नहीं मिली

मि मार्वेल ने कहा कि वह डरपोक है और अदृश्य आदमी का कोई भी काम उसके लिए बहुत मुश्किल होगा। उसने अदृश्य आदमी को यह बताने की कोशिश की कि वह असफल हो जाएगा। परंतु अदृश्य आदमी उसे जाने देने के लिए तैयार नहीं था।

मि मार्वेल का मन डर और आशंका से भरा हुआ था। मि मार्वेल को इस बात का डर परेशान करता रहता था कि पता नहीं अदृश्य आदमी उसे कौन-सा काम करने को कह दे।

Word Meaning

Timorously	– डरते हुए	Shattered	– टुकड़ों में
Wreckage	– तबाही	Rubicund	– लाल रंग का
Consternation	– चिंताएँ	Spasmodic	– अनियमित
Winced	– दु:ख व दर्द से दूर होना	Eloquent	– अच्छा वक्ता
Floundering	– अपरिपक्व होना	Yokels	– किसान
Slackened	– घटना	Ruddier	– गुलाबी रंग का
Stimulate	– उत्साह बढ़ाना	Funk	– भगदड़
Ineffectual	– असफल	Vigour	– ताकत
Gloaming	– गोधूलि बेला	Obsolete	– पुराना

Important Questions

Questions based on the Plot of the Chapter

Q 1. Mr Marvel tried to run away. What can be the possible reasons behind his trying to slip away?

मि मार्वेल ने भागने की कोशिश की। उनके भागने के पीछे संभावित कारण क्या हो सकते हैं?

मि मार्वेल का अदृश्य आदमी के लिए काम करना – मार्वेल का अदृश्य आदमी की किताबें लाने के लिए जाना – दोनों का आइपिंग से बाहर जाना – मार्वेल का भागने की कोशिश करना – अदृश्य आदमी का मानना कि मार्वेल द्वारा उसे धोखा मिला है – मार्वेल की भागने की इच्छा के पीछे कई कारण होना – उसकी आज़ाद जिंदगी पर बंदिश लगना – अदृश्य आदमी के कारनामे की वजह से पुलिस की कारवाई का डर – जनता की आँखों में चोर होने का भी भय होना – अदृश्य आदमी का साथ छोड़ने की इच्छा।

Ans. Mr Marvel was a man who was spotted by the Invisible Man as to be his helper. Mr Marvel was sent to the inn so that he could take the books and other important items for the Invisible Man. When the two were moving out of Iping after a long fury by the Invisible Man, they were talking about the future events. The Invisible Man had thought that Mr Marvel had tried to befool him and he wanted to run away leaving him behind. It was sure that Mr Marvel had an intention of running away. There were several reasons behind his running-away idea. He did not like to get stuck with the Invisible Man and do all his work.

Next, he was a carefree man and with the company of the Invisible Man, he could not lead the carefree life. Deeds of the Invisible Man were on every lips and soon it would be in the newspapers and it might have an effect upon Mr Marvel too.

He was fearing the prospects of actions by authority. He was in the eyes of the folks and they would never allow him to be the part of the social mainstream. Therefore, he was in the wish to slip away from the bad company of the Invisible Man.

Q 2. 'It will be in the papers!' What is the speaker referring to?

"यह अखबारों में होगा" वक्ता किसकी तरफ इंगित कर रहा है?

अजनबी के आने के दिन से ही उसका आइपिंग में चर्चा का विषय होना – उसकी हर गतिविधि व हरकत संदेहास्पद – मि हॉल का सेवा समाप्त कर देना – अजनबी का आइपिंग छोड़कर चले जाना – मार्वेल से मुलाकात होना – मार्वेल का धर्मशाला से किताबे चुराना – भीड़ द्वारा उसका पीछा करना – मार्वेल को बचाने के लिए अदृश्य आदमी का बीच में आना – अदृश्य आदमी का गुस्सा होना – आइपिंग में तबाही मचाना – पूरा आइपिंग खंडहर जैसा बना देना – यही खबर अखबार में निश्चित रूप से आने की संभावना जताना।

Ans. From the day of arrival, the strange man had been the talk of the town. All his deeds and appearance made the people talk about him. He was really in the lime light of the days that were passing on in Iping. After some days, things started to change and his services were curtailed by Mrs Hall.

This proved to be the start of the most interesting and peculiar events in Iping. He went out of Iping and then found a friend Mr Marvel whom he used as his messenger. Mr Marvel took out the books from the inn for the stranger and he was taken to be a thief. People ran behind him to catch him.

When people fail to get him through then they believe the coming of the strange man who was invisible then. The strange man had saved Mr Marvel and in the fury, he made a lot of damages in Iping. He had beaten the people mercilessly. Moreover, he had caused damage to the windows of the inn.

All these were to such an extent that Iping seems to be in the lap of ruins. This was expected to have the eyes of the newspapers and that's why, the man said that it all will be in the papers by next day of the event.

Q 3. Why do you think that the Invisible Man wanted an incompetent sidekick like Mr Marvel?

आपके अनुसार अदृश्य आदमी अपने लिए एक अयोग्य व्यक्ति को अपने साथी के तौर पर क्यों रखना चाहता था?

अदृश्य आदमी का आइपिंग से बाहर जाना – भोजन, कपड़े इत्यादि के लिए एक मददगार साथी की तलाश करना – मार्वेल एक सीधा तथा भोला इंसान – अदृश्य आदमी का उसको अपना साथी बनाने का निश्चय करना – मार्वेल में विरोधी स्वभाव का न होना – उसका आसानी से काम करने को सहमत होना – धमकी देकर उसको डराया जाना – इस वजह से अदृश्य आदमी का उसको अपना साथी बनाना।

Ans. When the Invisible Man was out of Iping, he was just helpless with his needs. He had no clothes, no food and no home to stay. He was in great need to have someone with him, who can make the ways out for him and as he spotted Mr Marvel, he found the man he required. In Mr Marvel, he saw a helping hand who would be of great use to him. Yet Mr Marvel was not very feasible to the expectations of the Invisible Man.

As Mr Marvel was slow, lethargic and weak too which was not sufficient for the kind of task that he was supposed to perform for the Invisible Man.

Even then the Invisible Man had believed on him because he wanted to dominate the man and none could be the best other than Mr Marvel. Mr Marvel had easily believed and easily been made to go for the work assigned by the Invisible Man.

Invisible Man had the idea that Mr Marvel may not rebel him easily and with the continuous threatening he could have him longer in his company. So, Mr Marvel was, even being a side kick, wanted by the Invisible Man.

Question based on the Character Sketch

Q 4. What impression do you form about Mr Marvel after reading the chapter?

इस पाठ को पढ़ने के बाद आप मि मार्वेल के बारे में क्या राय रखते हो?

मार्वेल एक साधारण इंसान – उसका एक प्रक्रति प्रेमी, सिद्धांतवादी व आजाद सोच वाला इंसान होना – अदृश्य आदमी से मिलने के दौरान उसका अपने दो जोड़ी जूतों के साथ व्यस्त होना – उसका बिना देखे ही अदृश्य आदमी से बातें करते रहना – उसका भविष्य की घटनाओं का भी अनुमान करना – उन्हें पता होना कि अजनबी के साथ रहने का परिणाम क्या हो सकता था – उनका डरपोक होना – अदृश्य आदमी की धमकी से डर जाना।

Ans. Mr Marvel was a man who represents simplicity at its best. He was a man who loves nature, was a carefree man and believes in his own principles and musings. He was the man who was as simple as sheep. When he met the Invisible Man, he was sitting near about a ditch with the two pair of shoes deciding which one to use. He was so lost in his thought that he fell in with the conversation which was with the Invisible Man and did not care to see even. When the conversation was almost over, he tried to see who was the man with him. This gives us the idea that how cool he was! He remained busy with his own meditations and often paid any heed to his surroundings.

He was having a good foresight too as he was aware of the consequences that he might meet when having association with Invisible Man. He was a timid person too and easily submitted to the threatening of the Invisible Man. He could not rebel him as he had threatened him with the extent of murder. He lacked the necessary courage in doing so, but he boldly pleaded the Invisible Man to set him free and allow him to go. In short use "comma" here.

Mr Marvel was simple, honest and a man who feared the authority, domination and power beyond.

14

At Port Stowe

Mr Marvel at Port Stowe

Mr Marvel and the Invisible Man reached Port Stowe. Mr Marvel looked quite worn-out. He had the Invisible Man's books beside him. He was very nervous and uncomfortable. He was nervously fumbling his various pockets over and again.

The Mariner Approaches to Mr Marvel

A mariner carrying a newspaper came out of the inn and sat down beside him. He initiated his introductory conversation by discussing about the pleasant wheather. Moreover, he heard the sound of coins near Mr Marvel and wondered how he got any money.

Mr Marvel Tried to Let out the Secret

Mr Marvel wondered from the mariner if there was anything else about the Invisible Man's aid in the newspaper. Confiding in the mariner, Mr Marvel resolved to share his secret of the Invisible Man with him. Bending towards the mariner, lowering the voice he disclosed that he knew certain things about the Invisible Man. Mr Marvel was about to tell his secret, suddenly his face expression changed. His face was eloquent of physical suffering. It was indeed the Invisible Man, who was giving physical torture to Mr Marvel for his attemp of betraying him.

Mr Marvel Lacked Manners

After getting hurt and realising that the Invisible man was near them, Mr Marvel rose up and called the news a hoax. The mariner wished to talk to him more, but Mr Marvel was in a hurry.

At Port Stowe

मि मार्वेल स्टॉव बंदरगाह पर

Mr Marvel (मि मार्वेल) और अदृश्य आदमी Port Stowe (स्टॉव बंदरगाह) पर पहुँचे। मि मार्वेल बहुत थके हुए से लग रहे थे। अदृश्य आदमी की किताबें भी उनके पास थीं। वह बहुत ही घबराए हुए और असहज थे। वह बार-बार व्याग्रता से अपनी जेबें टटोल रहा था।

नाविक का मि मार्वेल के पास आना

एक Mariner (समुद्री नाविक) हाथ में अखबार लिए Inn (सराय) से बाहर निकला और उनके पास आकर बैठ गया। उसने अपनी बातचीत Pleasant Wheather (खुशनुमा मौसम) के बारे में चर्चा करके शुरू की। हालाँकि, उसने मि मार्वेल के आस-पास से सिक्कों की आवाज भी सुनी और उसे आश्चर्य हुआ कि इस आदमी को धन कहाँ से मिला होगा।

मि मार्वेल का रहस्य बताने की कोशिश करना

मि मार्वेल ने नाविक से यह जानने की कोशिश की कि क्या अखबार में अदृश्य आदमी के बारे में कुछ और भी लिखा है। समुद्री नाविक पर भरोसा करते हुए मि मार्वेल ने अदृश्य आदमी का रहस्य उसे बताने का निश्चय किया। नाविक की ओर झुकते हुए तथा अपनी आवाज को धीमे करते हुए उन्होंने यह बात जाहिर की कि वह अदृश्य आदमी की कुछ बातें जानता हैं। मि मार्वेल रहस्य को बताने ही जा रहा था कि अचानक उनके चेहरे के भाव बदल गए। उनका चेहरा एक शारीरिक कष्ट को व्यक्त कर रहा था। यह वास्तव में अदृश्य आदमी ही था, जोकि मि मार्वेल को उसे धोखा देने के लिए Physical Torture (शारीरिक यातना) दे रहा था।

मि मार्वेल के अंदर संस्कार की कमी होना

अदृश्य आदमी द्वारा चोट पहुँचाने पर और यह आभास होने पर कि वह आस-पास ही है, मि मार्वेल वहाँ से उठकर जाने लगे और उन्होंने जाते-जाते यह कहा कि ये सारी खबरें अफवाह हैं। नाविक उनसे थोड़ी देर और बात करना चाहता था, परंतु मि मार्वेल जल्दी में थे।

The Mariner Realised the Truth

A friend of the mariner had seen money flying in thin air but was unable to get hold of it. Later, the mariner hears stories about a bunch of robberies and how people saw money just floating away. The truth dawned upon him.

नाविक को सच्चाई का पता चलना

नाविक के एक मित्र को हवा में Money (मुद्राएँ) उड़ते हुए दिखाई दी, लेकिन वह उसे पकड़ने में असमर्थ था। बाद में, नाविक को कई छोटी-बड़ी चोरियों का पता चला और उसने यह भी सुना था कि कैसे लोगों ने मुद्रा को उड़ते हुए देखा है। उसे सच्चाई का पता लगने लगा था।

Word Meaning

Weary – थका होना
Agitation – खीझ
Opulence – धन-संपदा
Altercation – विवाद करना
Inflicted – प्रदान करना
Cordon – पंक्तियाँ
Imperceptible – मुश्किल से दिखाई देना
Blimey – आश्चर्यजनक
Blarsted – बेवकूफ
Gait – चलना-फिरना
Dexterously – चालाकी से
Rouleaux – सिक्कों का पैकेट
Abandoned – परित्यक्त
Fumbling – लड़खड़ाना
Askew – तिरछा/टेढ़ा
Cast off – निकल पड़ना
Trespass – घुसपैठ करना
Tremendous – बहुत ज्यादा
Stiffly – बेतरतीब ढंग से
Stoutly – निडर होकर
Bandying – विवादित रूप से
Monologue – एक के द्वारा भाषण देना
Recriminations – आरोप लगाना
Collated – आभास होना

Important Questions

Questions based on the Plot of the Chapter

Q 1. Describe, in detail, the news published in the newspaper about the Invisible Man.

अदृश्य आदमी के बारे में अखबार में जो खबर छपी थी उसका विस्तार से वर्णन कीजिए।

अदृश्य आदमी और मार्वेल का आइपिंग से बाहर जाना – मि मार्वेल का धर्मशाला से किताबें लेने जाना – हक्सटर का मि मार्वेल को देखना – चोर होने का शोर मचाना – भीड़ द्वारा मार्वेल का पीछा करना – अदृश्य आदमी का हक्सटर व भीड़ को पीटना – मार्वेल को बचाना – अदृश्य आदमी द्वारा पूरे शहर को तोड़–फोड़ कर शमशान बना देना – अखबार में इसी घटना का वर्णन होना।

Ans. When the Invisible Man was about to leave Iping with his books and newly made friend Mr Marvel, Huxter noticed Mr Marvel as to be thief. On raising the alarm by Huxter, the folks of Iping went behind him and there was much hoax and panic. As Mr Marvel was with the books of the Invisible Man, so he was expected to get the help from the Invisible Man and it did happen. The Invisible Man came amidst of the folks and Mr Marvel. He started to beat Mr Huxter at first and then to the whole crowd.

There was a complete chaos and nobody could understand from where the blows were coming towards them. The crowd was dispersed by the incident and Mr Marvel made his escape. Now, as the crowd was infuriated by all those events, the Invisible Man started to have fun by beating them. He was doing it just for the satisfaction and he kept on doing the damage to them. He started to break the glass of the panes of the window and took a great pleasure in doing all this. As there was a massive ruin so it was obvious that the newspaper will have their eyes on it. That was the news published in the paper.

The Man Who was Running

The Peculiar Man is Running

In the early evening time, Dr Kemp was sitting in his study looking out of the window. He noticed a man running down the hill. He considered him to be a fool. Dr Kemp thought that he was also one of those who were haunted by the Invisible Man's mania.

एक विचित्र आदमी का दौड़ना

शाम के समय, डॉ केंप अपने अध्ययन कक्ष में में बैठे हुए थे और खिड़की से बाहर देख रहे थे। उन्होंने देखा कि पहाड़ी से दौड़ता हुआ एक आदमी नीचे आ रहा है। उन्हें लगा कि वह एक बेवकूफ इंसान है। डॉ केंप ने सोचा कि वह आदमी भी उनमें से एक है जो अदृश्य आदमी से बहुत डरे हुए थे।

The Invisible Man is Coming

Dr Kemp turned his attention away from the running man. But the people who observed Mr Marvel more closely could see the horror on his face. The onlookers were confused. After him, the sound of the running man came behind him, but there was no one visible. In a moment people realised that the Invisible Man was coming after him.

अदृश्य आदमी का आना

डॉ केंप ने भागते हुए आदमी से अपना ध्यान हटाया लेकिन जो लोग मि मार्वेल को करीब से देख रहे थे वे उनके चेहरे पर डर के संकेत देख सकते थे। लोग बिल्कुल समझने की स्थिति में नहीं थे। उनके पीछे-पीछे एक आदमी के दौड़ने की आवाज आ रही थी, परंतु वहाँ कोई नहीं था। लोग एक क्षण में ही समझ गए कि उनके पीछे अदृश्य आदमी आ रहा है।

Word Meaning

Albeit	– यद्यपि	Offence	– अपराध
Slender	– दुबला-पतला	Flaxen	– पीले रंग का
Blazing	– चमकते हुए	Verily	– वास्तव में
Spurted	– तेजी से	Occulted	– छिपाया जाना
Fugitive	– भागता हुआ	Abject	– भयानक

Important Questions

Question based on the Plot of the Chapter

Q 1. Why do you think that Mr Marvel was running for his life?

आपके अनुसार मि मार्वेल अपनी जान बचाने के लिए क्यों भाग रहे थे?

मि मार्वेल का जबरदस्ती अदृश्य आदमी की प्रत्येक बात मानना – अदृश्य आदमी का उनसे अपना काम कराना – मि मार्वेल का अदृश्य आदमी के कहने पर चोरी करना – आइपिंग के लोगों का उन्हें चोर समझना – अदृश्य आदमी द्वारा उनकी जान बचाना – नाविक के साथ बैठने पर राज खोलने की कोशिश करना – अदृश्य आदमी द्वारा पकड़े जाने पर बात बीच में ही छोड़ना – मार्वेल की नरकीय जिंदगी होना।

Ans. Mr Marvel was a friend cum helping hand for the Invisible Man. It was not by the choice but by force. Mr Marvel was compelled to do the work of the Invisible Man. If he would ever try to refuse the Invisible Man, he would have to face death at once. So, Mr Marvel was deeply disturbed. Mr Marvel had to leave his pleasant life and forced to make a robbery at the inn for his books. When he did so, people started running behind him for he was a thief.

He was saved by the Invisible Man though he did unlawful act. When he was sitting near the mariner he tried to let out the secret but could not do. He left the conversation in between due to the hurting from the Invisible Man.

That made him be called to be a mannerless fellow by the mariner. Yet, he was not the kind of man people took him to be, but he had to accept that. He thought his life had not been great and must have thought to make an escape.

In the "Jolly Cricketers"

Mr Marvel Enters the "Jolly Cricketers"

The people in the Jolly Cricketers inn were at ease, but then they heard the shouting in the street. The door was pushed open and Mr Marvel appeared, weeping and untidy, yelling for help. He attempted to shut the door as he was dead sure that the Invisible Man would kill him.

The People in the Inn are Courageous

The people in the inn were quite courageous. Firstly, they tried to calm Mr Marvel by ensuring him that he was safe and the doors were bolted. They were all ready to help him, but Mr Marvel was too much scared and ran here and there to find a place to hide.

The Invisible Man is Very Clever

There was rapping on the front door and then a window was smashed. The policeman wished that he had his truncheon with him. The plan was to let the Invisible Man try to enter from the front door. The man with the black- beard held his revolver to shoot the Invisible Man.

The Fighting Begin in the Inn

The window of the inn was suddenly smashed in and there was a screaming and yelling too and fro in the street. The Invisible man entered with a tremendous thud. He caught Mr Marvel. The black bearded man fired to rescue Mr Marvel and dragged him into the kitchen.

16

In the "Jolly Cricketers"

मि मार्वेल का "द जॉली क्रिकेटर्स" के अंदर जाना

The Jolly Cricketers (द जॉली क्रिकेटर्स) के अंदर खड़े लोग निश्चिंत थे और तभी उन्होंने सड़क पर चीखने-चिल्लाने की आवाज सुनी। दरवाजे को धक्का देकर खोला गया और Mr Marvel (मि मार्वेल), जोकि दिखने में गंदे थे और रो रहे थे, सहायता के लिए पुकारते हुए प्रकट हुए। उन्होंने दरवाजा बंद करने की कोशिश की, क्योंकि उन्हें पूरा विश्वास था कि Invisible Man (अदृश्य आदमी) उन्हें मार डालेगा।

सराय के लोगों का बहादुर होना

सराय के अंदर खड़े लोग बहुत बहादुर थे। पहले, उन लोगों ने मि मार्वेल को विश्वास दिलाया कि अब वह सुरक्षित हैं और सभी दरवाजे बंद हैं। वे सभी लोग उनकी मदद करने के लिए तैयार थे, परंतु मि मार्वेल अत्यधिक डरे हुए थे और छिपने का सही स्थान खोजने के लिए यहाँ-वहाँ भाग रहे थे।

अदृश्य आदमी का चालाक होना

दरवाजे पर दस्तक हुई और खिड़की को तोड़ दिया गया। पुलिसवाला अफसोस कर रहा था कि उसने अपनी Truncheon (लाठी) को साथ क्यों नहीं रखा था। योजना के अनुसार लोग यह चाहते थे कि अदृश्य आदमी सामने वाले दरवाजे से ही अंदर आए। Black-Beard (काली दाढ़ी) वाले आदमी ने अदृश्य आदमी को गोली मारने के लिए अपनी बंदूक निकाल ली।

सराय के अंदर लड़ाई शुरू हो जाना

सराय की खिड़की तोड़ दी गई और गली में इधर-उधर चीख-पुकार मच गई। अदृश्य आदमी बहुत तेज धमाके के साथ दाखिल हुआ। उसने मि मार्वेल को पकड़ लिया। काली दाढ़ी वाले आदमी ने मि मार्वेल को बचाने के लिए गोलियाँ चलाईं और उसे रसोई में खींच लिया।

Shots are Fired

The fight was on and the cabman got hold of the wrist of the Invisible Man. The policeman stamped on his foot and for the first time, the Invisible Man's voice was heard. Then he went out of the door and the others followed. The black-bearded man shot five bullets in the direction of the Invisible Man. There was silence. He thought that he had hit the Invisible Man.

गोलियाँ चलना

लड़ाई जारी थी और Cabman (वाहनचालक) ने अदृश्य आदमी के हाथ की कलाई पकड़ ली थी। पुलिसवाला उसके पैर पर चढ़ गया और पहली बार अदृश्य आदमी की आवाज वहाँ पर सुनाई दी। तभी वह भागकर दरवाजे से बाहर चला गया और लोग भी उसके पीछे भागने लगे। काली दाढ़ी वाले आदमी ने अदृश्य आदमी के भागने की दिशा में पाँच गोलियाँ चलाईं। चारों तरफ शांति थी। उसे लगा कि उसकी गोली अदृश्य आदमी को लग गई है।

Word Meaning

Anaemic	– कमजोर	Dishevelled	– गंदा
Convulsive	– तेज	Bawled	– चीखना
Staggering	– लड़खड़ाते हुए	Craning	– गर्दन आगे निकालना
Truncheon	– लाठी	Prowling	– चुपके से घूमना
Carving	– नक्काशी	Stabbed	– छिपी हुई चोट
Squeal	– चीख निकलना	Leveret	– खरगोश
Crumpled	– मरोड़ना	Reeling	– लड़खड़ाना
Blundered	– बड़ी गलती	Flails	– छड़ी से पीटना
Whooped	– चीखना	Obstinately	– जिद करना

Important Questions

Questions based on the Plot of the Chapter

Q 1. What plan was made by the people at the Jolly Cricketers to subdue the Invisible Man?

द जॉली क्रिकेटर्स में खड़े लोगों ने अदृश्य आदमी को हराने के लिए क्या योजनाएँ बनाई थीं?

मि मार्वेल का जान बचाने के लिए भागना – भागते हुए "द जॉली क्रिकेटर्स" में घुस जाना – लोगों से छिपने के लिए जगह माँगना – लोगों का उससे पूछना कि वह डरा हुआ क्यों है – लोगों को उस अदृश्य आदमी के बारे में पता चलना – लोगों द्वारा अदृश्य आदमी को पकड़ने के लिए योजनाएँ बनाना – सारे दरवाजे बंद कर देना – मुख्य दरवाजा खुला रखना – काली दाढ़ी वाले इंसान का बन्दूक लेकर तैयार रहना – पुलिसवाले का भी होना।

Ans. Mr Marvel was running for his life from the Invisible Man and he was frightened much. In order to save his life, he ran into the "Jolly Cricketers". The people who were at the bar asked Mr Marvel why he was so much disturbed and why he was running for his life. Mr Marvel told them to offer him a safe place at first so that he could hide himself.

People at the bar got the idea that it was the effect of the Invisible Man and they started to make and lay plans such that they could catch the Invisible Man. One of the men was with black-beard and he told that he would shoot the Invisible Man on his foot. Another told that he would hit him with a stick. Even the anaemic cabman was looking dangerous.

They planned to shut all the doors and bolt them but keeping the front door open to let him come into the inn and they would show him the treat. The policeman was standing there with them so that the Invisible Man could be handcuffed by him. Overall, everybody was a barrelful of beers and they were certain about their plan of catching the man. The thing that was important to see was the correct execution of the plan then.

Q 2. How did the struggle at "the Jolly Cricketers" end?
"द जॉली क्रिकेटर्स" में हो रहा संघर्ष कैसे समाप्त हो पाया?

मि मार्वेल का अपनी जान बचाने हेतु भागना – उसका "द जॉली क्रिकेटर्स" में प्रवेश करना – वहाँ के लोगों से मदद माँगना – अदृश्य आदमी का चुपके से धर्मशाला के अंदर आना – मि मार्वेल को घसीटते हुए रसोईघर की तरफ लाना – वाहनचालक द्वारा अदृश्य आदमी की कलाई पकड़ना – उसे एक मुक्के का प्रहार मिलना – काली दाढ़ी वाले आदमी द्वारा गोली चलाना, परंतु बेकार जाना – अदृश्य आदमी को अहसास होना कि शायद उसे निकलना चाहिए – उसका वहाँ से भागना – फिर से गोली चलना – संघर्ष का अंत होना।

Ans. When Mr Marvel was running for his life to be saved, he entered the inn, "The Jolly Cricketers". He was so afraid that he begged the people there to save his life from the Invisible Man and offer him a place to hide.

People at the inn consoled him not to get worried and stay calm as they assured him that they would not let him slip by this time and must hold him. They bolted all the doors of the house and were ready with the arms and all that.

When the Invisible Man made his entry from the back door and was dragging Mr Marvel towards the kitchen, it was the onset of the struggle at the inn.

He was dragging Mr Marvel and the cabman hold his wrist and cried, but a blow from somewhere ended his effort in vain. After it, the black-bearded man shot a fire, but it was not fruitful as it made no impact on the consequence.

The struggle was going on and the Invisible Man was attacked by the brave people. He realised that there was a little scope of a positivity for him here and made his escape through the main door.

As he did it, the black-bearded man shot more in the directions of his running, but it was in vain again. As he escaped, the struggle came to the end there.

Question based on the Character Sketch

Q 3. The people at "the Jolly Cricketers" were a bunch of brave men. What character traits are depicted by them?

"द जॉली क्रिकेटर्स" में खड़े लोग बहादुर व्यक्ति थे। उन्होंने कौन-सी चारित्रिक विशेषताओं का परिचय दिया था?

मि मार्वेल का जान बचाने के लिए भागना – जान बचाने के लिए सही जगह की खोज करना – मि मार्वेल का जान बचाने हेतु भागते हुए "द जॉली क्रिकेटर्स" में जाना – धर्मशाला के लोगों द्वारा उन्हें छिपने के लिए जगह देना – उन्हें सांत्वना देना – अदृश्य आदमी के खौफ को दरकिनार करते हुए धर्मशाला के लोगों का एक योजना बनाना – धर्मशाला के लोगों का बहुत ही साहसी होना – उन लोगों का बिना डरे अदृश्य आदमी का सामना करना – योजना पर मिलकर काम करना – उनका दृढ़निश्चयी होना।

Ans. When Mr Marvel was running for his life, he was in search of a place that could be very safe for him so that he could remain in his life. On his way to this jest, he entered "the Jolly Cricketers". At the inn, the people were really brave and they not only offered him the place to hide but they consoled him also.

They assured him that they would save him and most probably they would catch the Invisible Man. It was the bravery of the people at the inn that made them capable of having a plan otherwise the whole folks were having immense fear of his name.

The Invisible Man created a ruckus in the area that was closer to the surrounding and the residents would not be able to muster-up the courage to face the devastation that he could create there.

But, that was not the same with the people at "the Jolly Cricketers" and they showed the real strength by their endeavour of catching the Invisible Man. They believe that if they can remain as a unit and took care of the plan in a meticulous way, they would be able to avoid the misery from the Invisible Man.

Dr Kemp's Visitor

Ringing of the Door Bell

Dr Kemp was in his study when he heard shots being fired at the Jolly Cricketers(inn). He brushed it aside and went to his writing desk. After an hour, the front-door bell rang. Dr Kemp thought that it was a letter. Dr Kemp enquired and his maid replied that it was just a runaway ring. This made Dr Kemp restless.

The Blood Stains

It was two o' clock before Dr Kemp had finished his work. He rose, yawned and went downstairs to bed. After a while, he got thirsty and came to the kitchen. On his way down, he spotted a dark stain on the mat. It was drying blood. He was muddled with thoughts but returned to his room. When he came back, he was surprised to see a bloodstain on the door handle also.

The Invisible Man Reveals his Identity

In Dr Kemp's room, there was blood at many places and the sheets were torn. He heard a voice addressing him. Dr Kemp also saw a blood stained bandage hanging in mid air. He was advancing to grasp it but was stopped by a touch and a voice. The voice informed him that he was the Invisible Man. Initially, Dr Kemp had a hard time believing the voice. The Invisible Man introduced himself as Griffin.

17

Dr Kemp's Visitor

दरवाजे की घंटी का बजना

Dr Kemp (डॉ कैंप) अपने अध्ययन में थे, तभी उन्हें The Jolly Cricketers (द जॉली क्रिकेटर्स) Inn (सराय) में गोली चलने की आवाज सुनाई दी। उन्होंने इससे अपना ध्यान हटाया और वापस अपनी लिखने वाली टेबल के पास चले गए। एक घंटे के बाद, सामने के दरवाजे की घंटी बजी। डॉ कैंप को लगा कि उनके लिए पत्र आया होगा। डॉ कैंप ने अपनी नौकरानी से पूछा तो उसने बताया कि किसी ने शरारतपूर्वक घंटी बजाई थी। इस बात से डॉ कैंप बेचैन हो उठे।

खून के धब्बे

दो बजे तक डॉ कैंप ने अपना काम खत्म किया। वह उठे, उबासी ली और सोने चले गए। कुछ देर बाद उन्हें प्यास लगी और वे रसोईघर की तरफ आए। नीचे जाते हुए उन्होंने Mat (चटाई) पर एक गहरा Stain (धब्बा) देखा। वह सूखा हुआ खून था। वे सोच में पड़ गए, परंतु अपने कमरे की ओर वापस चले गए। जब वह वापस आए, तो उन्होंने दरवाजे के हेण्डल पर भी खून देखा।

अदृश्य आदमी का अपना परिचय देना

डॉ कैंप के कमरे में कई स्थान पर Bloodstains (खून के धब्बे) थे और चादर फटी हुई थी। उन्होंने उन्हें संबोधित करती हुई आवाज भी सुनी। डॉ. कैंप ने खून से सनी हुई एक पट्टी हवा में झूलती हुई भी देखी। वह उसे पकड़ने के लिए आगे बढ़े लेकिन एक स्पर्श और आवज ने उन्हें रोक दिया। आवाज ने उन्हें बताया कि वह Invisible Man (अदृश्य आदमी) है। प्रारंभ में, डॉ कैंप को उस आवाज पर विश्वास नहीं हो रहा था। डॉ कैंप को शांत करते हुए अदृश्य आदमी ने अपना परिचय Griffin (ग्रिफिन) के रूप में दिया।

Griffin Asks for Food and Clothing

Griffin told Dr Kemp that he was starving and asked for whisky, food and clothing. Dr Kemp was completely amazed. The things, happening in front of him were the insanest things ever happened in his life. Dr Kemp asked, how he became invisible, but Griffin kept dodging his questions.

ग्रिफिन का खाना और कपड़े माँगना

ग्रिफिन ने डॉ कैंप से कहा कि वह भूखा है और उसने विस्की, भोजन, तथा कपडों की माँग की, डॉ कैंप आश्चर्यचकित थे। उनके सामने जो कुछ भी हो रहा था, वह उनकी जिंदगी में पहले कभी भी नहीं हुआ था। डॉ कैंप ने उससे पूछा, कि वह अदृश्य कैसे हो गया लेकिन ग्रिफिन उनके सवाल से बचता रहा।

Griffin is too Tired

Griffin did mention Mr Marvel and tit-bits about the struggle at the inn and the subsequent shooting. Griffin further told Dr Kemp that he was too tired and wanted to rest. However, the thought of Dr Kemp deceiving him kept lurking in his mind.

ग्रिफिन का बहुत थका होना

ग्रिफिन ने Mr Marvel (मि मार्वेल) की चर्चा की और सराय में हुए संघर्ष और गोली चलने की घटना के बारे में बताया। ग्रिफिन ने डॉ कैंप को बताया कि वह बहुत थका हुआ है और आराम करना चाहता है। हालाँकि,उसके दिमाग में यह भी चल रहा था कि कहीं डॉ कैंप उसे धोखा न दे दें।

Word Meaning

Interstices – खुला हुआ
Facetted – कटना
Slackly – आलस्यपूर्ण
Shrillness – तेज आवाज
Astonishd – आश्चर्यचकित
Inquisitively – जिज्ञासु होना
Inklings – विचार
Reiterated – बार-बार करना
Rimly – कठोरता से
Albino – श्वेत वर्णमाला
Sane – समझदार
Pier – खंभा
Speculation – अनुमान
Resolutely – दृढ़ निश्चय
Quill – कलम
Trifle – कम होना
Superstitious – अंधविश्वासी
Eerie – डरावना
Frantic – उत्तेजित
Savagely – असभ्यतापूर्वक
Devilry – बुरा काम
Creaked – चरमराना

Important Questions

Questions based on the Plot of the Chapter

Q 1. Though he was a man of science, Dr Kemp also had inklings of superstition. Why did Dr Kemp grow superstitious?

डॉ केंप एक वैज्ञानिक थे पर उनमें भी अंधविश्वास झलकता था। उनमें अंधविश्वास कैसे आया?

डॉ केंप का वैज्ञानिक होना – डॉ केंप का एक यथार्थवादी सोच वाला इंसान होना – किसी भी मुद्दे को सोच-समझकर ही स्वीकार करना – अदृश्य आदमी के साथ मुलाकात होने पर उनका अंधविश्वासी हो जाना – कमरे के अंदर खून देखना – हवा में झूलती हुई पट्टी देखकर डॉ केंप का परेशान होना – वैज्ञानिक सोच होते हुए भी उनका मानना कि भूत होते हैं – प्रत्येक इंसान में अंधविश्वास का प्रमाण जरूर होना।

Ans. We know that Dr Kemp was a man of science, who had been rational in his approach. He would not take anything granted before judging it at his conscience and rationality. It is true that he believed on what he could see and perceive with his sense organs. But, it was not the case when he had his encounter with the Invisible Man. At the entry of the Invisible Man, Dr Kemp was unaware of his entry. When Kemp saw the blood spots, he came to know that something had been going away. He started to look for it as he was curious about it but found nothing. Suddenly Dr Kemp saw that a bandage that had been spattered with blood is hanging in the air.

Yet, he was a man of science but was not able to swallow what he had seen just. He thought either it was a trick or a way to hypnotise. He even thought the mere possibility of a ghost. A scientific man should not believe in all those rubbish, but there is a fact that human beings have often the element of superstition going with them.

The same was here with Dr Kemp. When the Invisible Man told his name, Dr Kemp didn't believe that it could be possible that a man could be invisible like the man he was facing.

Q 2. Why didn't Griffin answer all of Dr Kemp's questions?

ग्रिफिन ने डॉ केंप के सारे सवालों के उत्तर क्यों नहीं दिए?

मि मार्वेल का पीछा करते हुए ग्रिफिन का द जॉली क्रिकेटर्स में प्रवेश करना – ग्रिफिन का धर्मशाला के लोगों से संघर्ष होना – संघर्ष में ग्रिफिन को चोट लगना – उसकी वजह से खून निकलना – ग्रिफिन का कई दिनों से भूखा होना – ग्रिफिन को पर्याप्त नींद भी नहीं मिलना – ग्रिफिन का डॉ केंप के घर जाना – वहाँ डॉ केंप को उसका परिचय देना – डॉ केंप द्वारा ग्रिफिन से कई सवाल करना – ग्रिफिन का कुछ सवालों के उत्तर देना और कुछ के उत्तर न देना – डॉ केंप को कहना कि वह थका हुआ है, भूखा है और आराम करना चाहता है।

Ans. In the process of chasing Mr Marvel, Griffin entered the Jolly Cricketers from where he had to make his entry to the house of Dr Kemp.

He had a strong and bitter fight at the inn and in the process of dragging Mr Marvel, he had been injured by the jostle that occured there.

He was hurt badly and blood was flowing through the wound. He was very hungry for a couple of days because he had not been able to procure any food for himself. He had been deprived of sleep too and therefore restless he was.

In the meantime, he made his entry to the house of Dr Kemp and told him his name. Both had studied together in the college and when Kemp realised everything then as per in-built curiosity of a man of science, he began to ask him a number of question.

Some were answered and some were not answered. The reason behind that was the tiredness of the Invisible Man. He was hungry and sleep deprived too.

So, he requested Dr Kemp to allow him to have rest therefore some questions remain unanswered by the Invisible Man.

Question based on the Character Sketch

Q 3. Griffin was an insane scientist. What do you infer about his nature after reading the chapter?

ग्रिफिन एक बेतुका वैज्ञानिक था। इस पाठ को पढ़ने के बाद आप ग्रिफिन के बारे में किस निष्कर्ष पर पहुँचते हो?

ग्रिफिन का एक गुस्से वाला इंसान होना – उसका गैर-कानूनी काम करना और असामाजिक होना – विज्ञान का बेहतरीन जानकार होना – अपने आप को प्रतिभा के दम पर अदृश्य कर लेना – अपनी प्रतिभा का गलत इस्तेमाल करना – उसकी उम्मीद कि कोई उसकी मदद करे और उसका ख्याल रखे – भविष्य में उसके लिए बहुत कम उम्मीद होना।

Ans. From the very beginning of the incidents, the scientist Griffin had been a man of short temper, unsure and unlawful. From his story at Iping, he had proved himself to be just a man, who could never be social to any one.

He was a scientific genius and was very good at doing experiments. He made himself invisible and this was one of the examples of his talent. This was an extraordinary achievement.

But, unfortunately, what could have been very useful to the society, he used it in mannerless and purposeless way. He has to fight against the folks at Burdock and he injured himself.

When he met his class fellow, he expected a help from him. This shows how desperate he was for help from a man. It was his hunger and restlessness that forced him to seek for helping hand.

He was under immense pressure from the compulsion that he had with him. This chapter gives the idea that he had not much hope left in the coming time of his life.

The Invisible Man Sleeps

Griffin Threatens Dr Kemp

Dr Kemp assured Griffin that his freedom would be respected but still Griffin's mind was suspicious. Griffin kept all his options open and saw to it that his escape would be possible if the situation demanded. However, before going to sleep he threatened Dr Kemp. Dr Kemp was hurt that after giving his word, Griffin was thinking so.

Dr Kemp was still in doubt, but the Invisible Man was an undeniable fact. He tried to reason if such a thing was even possible. The investigation business went through the night. The servants woke up and Dr Kemp asked a breakfast to be laid for two. He was going through a dilemma. He wanted to inform someone about Griffin's presence, but then he had also given Griffin his promise.

ग्रिफिन का डॉ केंप को धमकाना

Dr Kemp (डॉ केंप) ने Griffin (ग्रिफिन) को विश्वास दिलाया कि उसकी आजादी को सम्मान दिया जाएगा, लेकिन अभी भी ग्रिफिन के दिमाग में शक था। ग्रिफिन ने चारों तरफ के विकल्पों को देखकर इस बात की तसल्ली कर ली कि अगर परिस्थितियाँ प्रतिकूल हो गई, तो वह भाग पाएगा या नहीं। हालाँकि, उसने डॉ केंप को सोने से पहले धमकी दी। डॉ केंप को इस बात का बुरा लगा कि उनके भरोसा देने के बाद भी, ग्रिफिन ऐसा सोच रहा था।

डॉ केंप अब भी संदेह की स्थिति में थे, परंतु अदृश्य आदमी एक Undeniable (निर्विवाद) सत्य था। उन्होंने यह जानने की कोशिश की कि क्या ऐसा संभव है। रात में जाँच-पड़ताल निरंतर रही। डॉ केंप ने नौकर से दो लोगों के लिए नाश्ता लगाने को कहा। वे दुविधा के माध्यम से गुजर रहे थे। वह ग्रिफिन की अपने घर में उपस्थिति को किसी को बताना चाहते थे, परंतु वे ग्रिफिन को अपना वादा दे चुके थे।

Word Meaning

Grotesque	– बदसूरत	Perish	– विनाश हो जाना
Hamper	– रुकावट पैदा करना	Preconceptions	– मान्यताएँ
Barred out	– फेंक देना	Flagrant	– बदनाम
Absurdity	– विसंगति	Ejaculating	– बोल उठना
Profound	– गहरा होना	Confronted	– सामना करना
Pallor	– पीलापन	Explicit	– स्पष्ट
Belvedere	– मीनार	Confine	– सीमित रखना

Important Questions

Questions based on the Plot of the Chapter

Q 1. Why was Griffin having a hard time trusting Dr Kemp?

ग्रिफिन को डॉ केंप पर भरोसा करने में इतना वक्त क्यों लग रहा था?

ग्रिफिन का मि मार्वेल को साथी बनाना और उनसे अपने काम निकलवाना– उन्हें चोरी करने पर मजबूर करना– मि मार्वेल का धमकी की वजह से सारे काम करना– मि मार्वेल का ग्रिफिन को चकमा देकर भागने की कोशिश करना– मि मार्वेल का ग्रिफिन द्वारा पीछा करते हुए डॉ केंप के घर तक आना – डॉ केंप से बात करने के बाद सोने की जगह माँगना – ग्रिफिन को डॉ केंप पर भरोसा न होना, क्योंकि मि मार्वेल ने भी उसे हाल में धोखा दिया था।

Ans. Griffin thought that Mr Marvel would be the most suitable for his purpose. He made Mr Marvel to rob in the inn for his books and Mr Marvel did it reluctantly. Mr Marvel was doing all this by force and not by choice. Mr Marvel had to do that because he was threatened to death.

He wanted to leave this job because he didn't like it and he was feeling the risk of it in coming time. He tried to disclose the facts to the mariner about Griffin, but he failed in doing so. He was chased to a bitter end by Griffin that lead both to Burdock. Here, Mr Marvel was saved by the brave people at 'the Jolly Cricketers'. Suddenly, Griffin made his way to his classmate Dr kemp, who lived the same place. Griffin entered his house and after long course of conversation, Dr Kemp offered him food, clothes and shelter but there was a doubt in his mind that what would he do if Dr Kemp betrayed him. He could not trust anyone as Mr Marvel had cheated him recently.

Certain First Principles

Griffin's Secret is Out

Dr Kemp came running to Griffin's room and enquired about the smashing sound. Griffin told that it was his wounded arm which was giving him trouble. Dr Kemp further informed him that his secret was in the newspapers. People knew about his existence.

Griffin Explains his Invisibility

Dr Kemp said that if Griffin needed his help then, he must give him some details about his transparent form. Griffin starts narrating the incidents that led him to make this discovery. Initially, he was a medical student but Griffin switched to physics because light fascinated him.

Griffin Keeps Researching in Secret

Griffin left London (and University College) six years ago and went to Chesilstove, where he was a teacher and a student. He had the idea in his mind and started developing it from there. But he had to keep his research a secret as his professor was a thief of ideas. He didn't want to lose the credit for his own research. He never mentioned his research to anyone.

Griffin Gets a Breakthrough

One night, he discovered the methodology of making a human invisible. His joy knew no bounds. After three years of teaching and research, he didn't have the money, he needed to complete his research. So, he resorted to thievery and robbed his father. This money he had stolen belonged to someone else. Unable to bear the aspersion, his father shot himself dead.

Certain First Principles

ग्रिफिन का राज खुल जाना

Dr Kemp (डॉ कैंप) भागते हुए Griffin (ग्रिफिन) के कमरे की तरफ पहुँचे और टूटने की आवाज के बारे में पूछताछ की। ग्रिफिन ने बताया कि यह उसके जख्मी हाथ के कारण हुआ था जोकि उसे परेशान कर रहा था। डॉ कैंप ने उसे यह सूचना दी कि उसके सारे रहस्य अखबार में छप चुके हैं। लोग उसकी हकीकत जान चुके थे।

अपनी अदृश्यता का ग्रिफिन द्वारा वर्णन करना

डॉ कैंप ने ग्रिफिन से कहा कि अगर वह उनकी मदद चाहता है, तो उसे अपनी अदृश्यता के बारे में बताए। ग्रिफिन ने सारी घटनाओं का वर्णन करना शुरू किया, जिसकी वजह से उसने इस आविष्कार को अंजाम दिया। प्रारंभ में, वह मेडिकल विद्यार्थी था लेकिन उसने Physics (भौतिक विज्ञान) विषय ले लिया क्योंकि उसकी प्रकाश में रुचि थी।

गुप्त रूप से ग्रिफिन का अपने शोधकार्य को जारी रखना

ग्रिफिन छः वर्ष पूर्व London (लंदन) and University College (और विश्वविद्यालय) छोड़कर Chesilstove (चेसिलस्टॉव) चला गया, जहाँ पर वह एक अध्यापक और एक छात्र था। उसके दिमाग में एक विचार था और उसने वहीं पर उस पर काम करना शुरू कर दिया परंतु उसे अपने शोध को गुप्त रखना पड़ा। क्योंकि उसके Professor (प्राध्यापक) विचारों के चोर थे। वह अपने शोधकार्य का श्रेय किसी और को नहीं देना चाहता था। उसने कभी भी अपने शोध के बारे में किसी को नहीं बताया था।

ग्रिफिन को सफलता मिल जाना

एक रात, उसने इंसान को अदृश्य बनाने का तरीका खोज लिया। उसकी खुशी की सीमा न रही। लगातार तीन सालों तक पढ़ाने और शोधकार्य करने के पश्चात्, उसके पास अपने शोध को पूरा करने के लिए धन नहीं था। उसे चोरी करनी पड़ी और उसने अपने पिता का धन ही चुरा लिया। जो धन उसने चुराया था वह किसी और का था। चोरी के Aspersion (कलंक) को उसके पिता बर्दाश्त न कर सके और स्वयं को गोली मार ली।

Word Meaning

Serviette	– रूमाल	Glimmering	– चमकते हुए
Elusively	– पकड़ में न आने वाला	Meshes	– जाल
Suffices	– जरूरतें	Frightful	– डरावनी
Bounder	– दुष्ट	Instinct	– इरादा
Prying	– जासूसी करना	Knavish	– बेईमान
Incredulous	– भरोसा न होना	Gaping	– खुला हुआ
Overwhelming	– बहुत तेज (खुशी होना)	Splendid	– शानदार
Transcend	– श्रेष्ठ होना	Shabby	– फटेहाल अवस्था
Hemmed-in	– बंद रहना	Provincial	– प्रांतीय

Important Questions

Questions based on the Plot of the Chapter

Q 1. Chesilstove was the place that changed Griffin's life. Elaborate.

चेसिलस्टॉव ने कैसे ग्रिफिन की जिंदगी बदल दी?

ग्रिफिन का लंदन के कॉलेज से पढ़ाई पूरी करना – कॉलेज दिनों में चिकित्सक विद्यार्थी होना – भौतिक विज्ञान की तरफ आकर्षण बढ़ जाना – विषय परिवर्तन कर लेना – चेसिलस्टॉव के एक प्रांतीय कॉलेज में प्रोफेसर बन जाना – अपना शोध जारी रखना – एक दिन शोध का पूरा होना – ग्रिफिन का अदृश्य होने वाले सूत्र की खोज कर लेना – उसका स्वप्न पूरा हो जाना – अतः यह कहना उचित कि चेसिलस्टॉव ने उसकी जिंदगी की दिशा व दशा बदल दी।

Ans. Griffin was greatly devoted to the experiment that he was carrying but after completion of his college he had left London. In his college days, he was a student of Chemistry and medical field but he developed a keen interest in Physics and specially in light. It was a switch over in his studies. He also wanted to pursue his experiment in a way that no one could get a hint of it. For it, he made a change in the place.

He left London for good and shifted himself to a place named Chesilstove where he joined a provincial college as a professor and side by side he kept on going with his experiment. He burnt the mid-night oil for having the desired success.

In the end, that fine moment arrived one night when he was experimenting in his laboratory. He got the formula that would make the human body inivisible completely. It was his ever been cherished dream and when he fulfilled it there was no bounds to his joy. He had done with his discovery and that's why it can be said that Chesilstove was the place that changed his life all the way.

Q 2. What was Griffin's theory regarding invisibility?

अदृश्यता के बारे में ग्रिफिन की थ्योरी क्या कहती है?

ग्रिफिन द्वारा डॉ केंप को अपनी अदृश्यता के बारे में बताया जाना – ग्रिफिन का कहना कि कोई चीज दिखती तभी है जब प्रकाश उसकी सतह से परावर्तन के बाद लौटता है – परावर्तन न हो तो कोई भी चीज नहीं दिखती – ग्रिफिन ने शरीर के अपवर्तनांक को इतना कम कर दिया कि शरीर अदृश्य दिखाई देने लगा – मूलभूत तथ्यों से ही पूरा शोध तैयार करना।

Ans. When Griffin was having a talk with Dr Kemp he was asked to explain how did he manage to make his body inivisible. To this question, Griffin gave a wonderful explanation to Dr Kemp. This explanation was full of surprises yet it was such a truth that scientists had paid no attention to it ever.

Griffin gave a detailed explanation to Dr Kemp. He started with explaining how a body can be visible. A body is visible only when light gets reflected through it. Light has three basis properties- it can reflect, refract or gets absorbed by the surface.

Visibility is the function of reflection. Griffin told him further that if no light is reflected from the surface of a body then it won't be visible. So, what comes out as a fact, is lowering the refractive index can do the trick.

Griffin let him know that he had done the same in his experiments. He lowered the refractive index of human body and it was the same consequence that made it invisible. This was the theory of Griffin regarding his invisibility. With this impressive explanation, Dr Kemp was amazed yet these were the basics.

At the House in Great Portland Street

Griffin Goes to Bury his Father

Griffin had stolen his father's money which led to his suicide. But Griffin was not feeling sorry for his father. When he went to bury him, he didn't even try to save his character and thought that the father was himself responsible for everything. However, walking down the old streets reminded him of the past things.

The First Success

Griffin reiterates his point before Dr Kemp that the other details are in the three books and thus they are very important. Griffin's first experiment was a bit of white wool fabric. When it vanished, Griffin could hardly believe it.

Griffin Makes a Cat Invisible

A cat appeared on his window and Griffin thought that he had got another thing to experiment with. He administered the invisibility drug, on the cat, but the experiment failed on two counts.

The claws and the tapetum the pigment stuff at the back of the eye were still visible. Then an old woman heard cat sounds and came in search of her. She suspected Griffin of experimenting on animals.

At the House in Great Portland Street

ग्रिफिन का अपने पिता को दफनाने के लिए जाना

Griffin (ग्रिफिन) ने अपने पिता के पैसे चुराए थे, जिसकी वजह से उसके पिता ने खुदकुशी कर ली थी। परंतु ग्रिफिन को अपने पिता की मौत का कोई अफसोस नहीं था। जब वह उन्हें दफनाने गया तब भी उसने अपने चरित्र का बचाव करने की कोशिश नहीं की और वह यही सोचता रहा कि उसके पिता अपनी मौत के लिए स्वयं जिम्मेदार थे। हालाँकि पुरानी गलियों से लौटते समय उसको अपने पुराने दिन भी याद आ रहे थे।

पहली सफलता

ग्रिफिन ने Dr Kemp (डॉ केंप) के सामने अपने शब्दों को दोहराया कि उसकी अन्य महत्त्वपूर्ण चीजें उन तीन किताबों में हैं और इसलिए वे उसके लिए बहुत महत्त्वपूर्ण हैं। ग्रिफिन ने अपना पहला प्रयोग White Wool (सफेद ऊन) पर किया था। जब वह अदृश्य हो गया, तो वह इस पर मुश्किल से विश्वास कर पाया।

ग्रिफिन का एक बिल्ली को अदृश्य करना

ग्रिफिन को खिड़की पर एक बिल्ली दिखाई दी और वह सोचने लगा कि उसको शोध के लिए एक और चीज मिल गई है। उसने अदृश्यता की दवा बिल्ली को पिलाई, लेकिन उसका प्रयोग दो बातों से असफल हो गया।

बिल्ली के पंजे और उसकी आँखों के पीछे मौजूद Tapetum (टेपटम) नाम का Pigment (पिगमेन्ट) अभी भी दृश्य था। तभी एक Old Woman (वृद्ध महिला) वहाँ आई और बिल्ली की आवाज सुनकर उसे ढूंढने लग गई। उसे शक था कि ग्रिफिन जानवरों पर कोई प्रयोग कर रहा है।

Griffin has a Fight with the Landlord

The next day, Griffin remembers quite clearly. Though he was within touching distance of his dream, he was not excited. The landlord came asking for rent and making many enquiries. The old woman had probably told him about the cat. The landlord also thought that Griffin's behaviour was curious. He peeped into the room and Griffin thought that his research was in danger. Griffin loses his temper and he throws the landlord out.

Griffin Decides to Vanish

After the fight with the landlord, there was a crisis situation. Griffin knew that he would be thrown out and he had so little money to find a new apartment. Moreover, he had to move the apparatus. He prepared by sending his three books and a cheque book to the nearby post-office from where he could collect them later.

Griffin : The Invisible Man

Griffin was under the influence of drugs when the landlord came with a legal notice. Griffin opened the door and the landlord was left frightened as his face had turned white. The night was painful and agonising.

His skin was on fire and Griffin had never expected this suffering. Griffin held on till the end and somehow survived the transformation. When he woke up later, his strength had returned.

Griffin Dismantles the Apparatus

Griffin started to dismantle the apparatus as there was rapping on the door. He was near the window when the door was banged. But it didn't open due to the locks. The landlord, his two step-sons and the old lady entered only to find the place empty. The landlord agreed with the old woman that Griffin was a vivisectionist while his sons said that he was an electrician as there were Dynamos in the room. Later, Griffin smashed the radiators also.

ग्रिफिन की उसके मकान मालिक से लड़ाई होना

ग्रिफिन को अगला दिन बहुत अच्छी तरह याद था। वह अपने सपने के पूरा होने के बिल्कुल करीब था, पर वह बिल्कुल भी उत्साहित नहीं था। Landlord (मकान मालिक) किराया लेने आया और उसने आते ही बहुत सारे प्रश्न पूछे। बूढ़ी औरत ने मकान मालिक को उस बिल्ली के बारे में बता दिया था। मकान मालिक को भी ग्रिफिन का व्यवहार अजीब लगता था। उसने उसके कमरे में हर जगह झाँकना शुरू कर दिया था और ग्रिफिन को लगा कि उसका शोध अब खतरे में है। ग्रिफिन को बहुत गुस्सा आया और उसने मकान मालिक को कमरे से बाहर फेंक दिया।

ग्रिफिन का गायब होने का फैसला करना

मकान मालिक से लड़ाई होने के बाद स्थिति बुरी हो गई थी। ग्रिफिन को पता था कि अब उसे बाहर निकाल दिया जाएगा और उसके पास नए मकान के लिए पर्याप्त धन नहीं था। इसके अलावा उसे अपने सारे Apparatus (यंत्रों) को भी हटाना होगा। उसने अपनी तीन किताबों और एक चेकबुक को पास के डाकघर में भिजवा दिया, जहाँ से वह उनको बाद में ले सकता था।

ग्रिफिन : एक अदृश्य आदमी

ग्रिफिन Drugs (ड्रग्स) के प्रभाव में था, जब मकान मालिक एक कानूनी नोटिस लेकर आया। ग्रिफिन ने दरवाजा खोला और मकान मालिक उसके सफेद चेहरे को देखकर डरकर भाग गया। पूरी रात दर्द व पीड़ा से युक्त थी।

उसकी त्वचा जल रही थी और ग्रिफिन ने कभी भी इस पीड़ा का अनुमान नहीं किया था। ग्रिफिन ने अंत तक इस पीड़ा को बर्दाश्त किया और किसी तरह से उसने अपने शरीर में हो रहे इस परिवर्तन का सामना किया। जब वह सो कर उठा, तो उसकी ताकत वापस आ चुकी थी।

ग्रिफिन का अपने यंत्रों को नष्ट कर देना

ग्रिफिन के कमरे के दरवाजे पर लगातार दस्तक हो रही थी और वह अपने सारे यंत्रों को नष्ट करने के काम में लगा हुआ था। जब दरवाजा जोर से खींचा गया वह खिड़की के पास था। कुंडी व ताला लगे होने के कारण यह नहीं खुला। मकान मालिक, उसके दो सौतेले बेटे और बूढ़ी महिला कमरे के अंदर गए, तो पता चला कि कमरा खाली है। मकान मालिक उस बूढ़ी महिला से सहमत था कि ग्रिफिन ने जानवरों पर शोध किया है और उसके बेटे यह मान रहे थे कि वह तो बिजली का काम करने वाला था, क्योंकि उसके कमरे में कुछ Dynamo (डायनेमो) मिले थे। बाद में ग्रिफिन ने अपने सारे यंत्रों को तोड़ दिया था।

Griffin Sets Fire to the House

Griffin remained downstairs while the others argued about him. He had already planned to burn everything in his room and took a box of matches. He also set the gas on. He fired the house. Dr Kemp was shocked. Griffin justified the act by saying that it was the only way to cover his trail. Now, Griffin was invisible and could do anything without the fear of being caught.

ग्रिफिन का घर में आग लगा देना

जब अन्य लोग ग्रिफिन की चर्चा कर रहे थे तो वह चुपचाप नीचे बैठा हुआ था। उसने अपने कमरे के सारे सामान में आग लगाने की योजना बना ली, और उसने हाथ में माचिस का डिब्बा लिया। उसने गैस को भी जलता हुआ छोड़ दिया। उसने अंततः घर में आग लगा दी। Dr Kemp (डॉ. कैंप) को बहुत ज्यादा आश्चर्य हुआ। ग्रिफिन ने यह कहकर अपने कृत्य को सही ठहराया कि यह उसके राज को छिपाए रखने का एकमात्र उपाय था। इस समय तक ग्रिफिन अदृश्य हो गया था और पकड़े न जाने के डर से वह कुछ भी कर सकता था।

Word Meaning

Thicket – झाड़ी
Scant – सस्ता
Desecrated – बर्बाद हो जाना
Rank – बदबूदार
Sordid – अनैतिक
Desolate – वीरान
Cypher – बिना किसी मूल्य के
Opium – अफीम
Seethe – गुस्से से भरा
Iridescent – चमकदार (बहुरंगा)
Grating – परेशानी
Apathetic – विचार शून्य
Strychnine – एक प्रकार का पदार्थ
Invigorated – ऊर्जा से भरा हुआ
Protest – विरोध
Quivering – काँपना
Crisis – संकट की स्थिति
Drowsy – नींद में होना
Blundering – चूक कर देना
Funeral – दाह संस्कार करना
Tinkered – मरम्मत करने वाला
Rubble – कचरा
Gaunt – पतला
Cant – परंपरा
Inanity – बेवकूफी
Wreath – घेरना
Clamped – जोर से पकड़ना
Sinews – नस
Bustle – चहल-पहल होना
Inconclusive – अनिर्णायक
Transient – बदलता हुआ
Flabbiness – इधर-उधर लटकता हुआ
Tormenting – उत्पीड़न
Jabber – बकवास करना
Fuss – हंगामा करना
Glared – चमकना
Writ – याचिका
Racking – गहरा

Important Questions

Questions based on the Plot of the Chapter

Q 1. Why was the landlord curious about Griffin's work?

मकान मालिक ग्रिफिन के कार्य को लेकर ज्यादा उत्सुक क्यों था?

ग्रिफिन का शोध अजीबोगरीब होना – हमेशा सबसे अलग रहना – ग्रिफिन का अपने शोध के साथ व्यस्त रहना – ग्रिफिन के कमरे में शोध के सामान अजीबोगरीब ढंग के और अजीब आवाजें करने वाले थे – ग्रिफिन द्वारा एक बिल्ली के ऊपर अपना शोध करना – बिल्ली की आवाज सुनकर मकान मालिक का ऊपर आना – ग्रिफिन को शक की नजर से देखना – ग्रिफिन की हरकतें संदेह के दायरे में ही रहती थीं इसलिए मकान मालिक का उस पर शक करना और उत्सुक रहना।

Ans. Griffin had a room in the Portland Street. He was purposed there for his experiment and the experiment was supposed to make an Invisible Man. Griffin, as his nature was, remains desolated always busy with his apparatus and experiments.

There was no limit to the timings of his work and he was crazy about it and wanted to complete his experiment as soon as it could be. There were many tantranums that were lying in the room of Griffin. When Griffin was able to make the wool invisible, he was very happy and tried to perform the same on a cat.

Fortunately, a cat entered his room and then Griffin got hold of it and started an experiment on it. He got another interruption from his landlord saying that he had a doubt that there's an experiment being performed on an animal.

Every now and then Griffin would do some sort of thing that would leave everyone curious and the same had happened then. The apparatus that Griffin used to his experiments reflect another dubious aspect about him. These things were very unusual and the impression that Griffin leaves all the time calls the suspicion from the landlord.

Q 2. "But this brought matters to a crisis". Was Griffin himself responsible for the crisis that he was confronted with?

लेकिन इससे मामला और बिगड़ गया। क्या ग्रिफिन खुद मामला बिगाड़ने के लिए जिम्मेदार था?

ग्रिफिन के रहने वाले कमरे का प्रयोगशाला भी होना – ग्रिफिन का प्रयोग दूसरों के लिए कौतूहल का विषय – मकान मालिक का ग्रिफिन के कमरे में आना – बिल्ली के ऊपर प्रयोग करने के विषय में पूछना – ग्रिफिन का उत्तर न देना – ग्रिफिन को एक बड़ी सफलता मिलना – उसका अदृश्यता का प्रयोग खुद पर ही करना – प्रयोग के प्रभाव में मकान मालिक के लिए दरवाजा खोल देना – मकान मालिक का उसके सफेद चेहरे को देखकर डर जाना – मकान मालिक का डरकर भाग जाना और अगले दिन पूछताछ करना – ग्रिफिन को गुस्सा आना और उसका मकान मालिक को बाहर फेंक देना – ग्रिफिन के लिए मुसीबत की शुरूआत होना।

Ans. The house in which Griffin was living, was not only his residence but it was a lab for him, where he was performing his experiment. There was a whole lot of apparatus in the room and all set-up were established in a fine way.

When he was going on smoothly with his experiment, he managed to vivisect a cat that made his landlord curious about him and he was enquiring about it. When the landlord didn't get the details of it. He started to have a keen eye on Griffin and this made Griffin very much furious.

He was in a rage when being enquired frequently, but kept himself cool because he was on the verge of the breakthrough in his experiment.

One day when Griffin was under the influence of the drug then his door was knocked and when the door was opened his face was so white that the landlady ran away downstairs in utmost fright.

After the event, the landlord demanded the rent and made a lot of enquiries about his work that was enough to provoke Griffin. In a rage, he just threw out his landlord out of his room and it was why the matter had been to a crisis.

Q 3. The transformation was agonisingly painful for Griffin.

शारीरिक परिवर्तन ग्रिफिन के लिए अति दर्दनाक था। इसका वर्णन करें।

कॉलेज छोड़ने के बाद ग्रिफिन का विषय में परिवर्तन करना – रसायन विज्ञान को छोड़कर भौतिक विज्ञान की तरफ आकर्षण होना – शोध के लिए रूपये की जरूरत होना – अपने पिता के रूपये चुराना – ग्रिफिन के पिता का आत्म हत्या करना – ग्रिफिन का अदृश्यता के ऊपर शोध करना – बिल्ली पर शोध करना – प्रयोग सफल रहना – ग्रिफिन की सफलता – ग्रिफिन का अदृश्यता का प्रयोग खुद पर दोहराना – प्रयोग में एक विशेष ड्रग का सेवन करना – शारीरिक परिवर्तन के दौर से गुजरना – परिवर्तन के दौरान शरीर में बहुत कष्ट व पीड़ा का अनुभव होना – घंटों तक इस कष्ट से गुजरना – ग्रिफिन की पीड़ा इसी कारण से।

Ans. After leaving the college, Griffin changed the field of his study. He left Chemistry for the sake of optics and started his experiment in the same field. For meeting the expenses of his experiment he made a robbery of money from his own father.

This resulted to a bad consequence leading to the suicide of Griffin's father, but he didn't care about it. Such was the height of his dream. For this he had worked hard, burnt the mid-night oil and a lot more he had done. He experimented on a cat first to confirm the validity of experiment.

He was on the high side when the validity of his experiment came true. There was no bounds to the happiness of Griffin. It was the high time when Griffin was about to do the experiment on him. The experiment consists of a rare drug to be swallowed by the person, who was supposed to be invisible.

Griffin swallowed that rare drug that made him suffer a lot of pain because the drug started to burn his skin. This burning sensation was agonisingly painful as it sets a process of transformation inside the body of the subjected. The same was happening with Griffin then.

Q 4. Why did Griffin dismantle his apparatus and burn down the house?

ग्रिफिन ने अपने सभी सामानों को तबाह क्यों कर दिया था और घर में आग क्यों लगा दी थी?

ग्रिफिन का रसायन विज्ञान के विषय में मेधावी विद्यार्थी होना – बाद में भौतिक विज्ञान की तरफ आकर्षण होना – ग्रिफिन का अदृश्यता के ऊपर शोध करना – उसका सफल प्रयोग बिल्ली के ऊपर करना – प्रयोग की सफलता को अपने ऊपर भी दोहराना–ग्रिफिन का कार्य सिद्ध हो जाना – उसे अब अपने किसी सामान की जरूरत न होना – मकान मालिक द्वारा ग्रिफिन को घर खाली करने को बोलना – ग्रिफिन का नाराज हो जाना – नाराजगी की वजह से घर में आग लगा देना – सामान की कोई परवाह न करना, क्योंकि उसकी कोई आवश्यकता नहीं रही।

Ans. Griffin was a brilliant student in Chemistry, but later on he switched his interest to Physics and optics. He was determined to develop such a formula that could lead to the state of invisibility.

His only dream was to be invisible. For this, he started performing many experiments and he gathered many apparatus and rented a room in the great Portland Street.

He experimented on a cat first. When he realised that experiment could be successful he wanted to try the same on himself. Experiment consisted of swallowing a drug that resulted into the transformation of a body.

When the experiment was in mid way then landlord knocked the door and Griffin appeared in a state of perplex to his landlord. On seeing the appalling face the landlord was so frightened and ordered Griffin to vacate his premise.

Griffin had completed the transformation process and he didn't need his apparatus more. The rage over his landlord made him set fire in the house alongwith his apparatus too.

Q 5. The insane scientist was obsessed with his discovery and wanted to hide it at any cost. In the process he lost all moral values and his conscience. In the light of this statement, attempt a character sketch of Griffin.

ग्रिफिन किसी भी तरह अपने शोध को और उसकी गुप्तता को बचाने के लिए पागलपन की हद तक था। ऐसा करने के लिए उसने नैतिक मूल्यों और सुविचार को छोड़ दिया था। इस कथन का संदर्भ लेते हुए ग्रिफिन का चरित्र चित्रण करें।

कोई शक नहीं था कि ग्रिफिन एक मेधावी विद्यार्थी है – रसायन विज्ञान में बेहतरीन होना– परंतु बाद में भौतिक विज्ञान की तरफ आकर्षण होना – ग्रिफिन का प्रयोग उसके लिए महत्त्वपूर्ण होना – प्रयोग का सफल होना – प्रयोग में लगने वाले पैसे के लिए पिता के पैसे चोरी करना – पिता की मौत पर दु:खी न होना – बिल्ली पर प्रयोग गैरकानूनी था – अपने प्रयोग की जानकारी किसी को नहीं होने देना – ग्रिफिन का नैतिक तौर पर पतन होना – उसे किसी भी बात की परवाह न होना – ग्रिफिन एक न्यायशून्य व विवेकशून्य इंसान होना।

Ans. No doubt about the fact that Griffin was a brilliant scientist. Griffin was really obsessed with the Science. He was a brilliant of Chemistry and later on proved it in optics too. He discovered such a drug that made him invisible.

This was all the instances of his scientific brilliancy but there was an aspect of him that never deserved appreciation. That aspect was his moral values that he never cared of. In his experiment, he needed a lot of money and he never minded robbing his father.

Consequently, his father shot himself dead but there was no regret for Griffin. Such was his craze about Science. He didn't mind vivisection even that was illegal in the country. Manners and behaviour were also out of sorts for him.

He never intended to be social with anyone. He wanted none to know about his experiment because his purpose was to get an impunity without any obstruction from others. So, it can be well said that the height of the character was not there for Griffin anyway.

In Oxford Street

Griffin Gets Extraordinary Advantage

Griffin was overjoyed and exalted. He felt like a seeing man in the city of blind. But the moment he emerged upon Great Portland Street, he was hit violently behind by a passer by who in turn was highly astonished to find no one there.

Griffin Realises the Disadvantages

A cabman rushed to catch the basket and his hands met Griffin's neck. Griffin was hurt and the crowd rushed to the scene. Griffin ran away from the place. On the street, his feet got stamped, his shoulder got bruised and most of all, he was stark naked and thus caught a cold.

Griffin Grows Helpless

Griffin's initial happiness had flown away and he thought how he was going to get out of the mess he was in. He was feeling so helpless that he nearly cried. Then a dog traced him. Griffin realised that the dog could smell him. Griffin was again in danger of being discovered and ran away.

Footprints Without Feet

A procession was coming his way and Griffin thought that he will not be able to go through them. Moreover, he did not want to get away from his house. He ran up the white steps of a house and left muddy foot prints on the newely whitened steps. Two little children noticed his imprints. The fear of being caught paralyzed Griffin, but somehow he was able to give them a slip.

In Oxford Street

ग्रिफिन को विशेष लाभ की प्राप्ति होना

अदृश्य होने के बाद Griffin (ग्रिफिन) अत्यधिक प्रसन्न था। वह ऐसा महसूस कर रहा था जैसे वह अंधों के शहर में देखने वाला आदमी हो। लेकिन जैसे ही वह Great Portland Street (ग्रेट पोर्टलैण्ड स्ट्रीट) से निकला तभी एक राहगीर बहुत तेजी से उससे टकरा गया और किसी को वहाँ न देखकर बहुत हैरान हो गया।

ग्रिफिन को कमियाँ महसूस होना

एक Cabman (वाहनचालक) ने टोकरी को पकड़ने की कोशिश की, परंतु उसके हाथ में ग्रिफिन की गर्दन आ गई। ग्रिफिन को चोट लगी थी और उस जगह एक भारी भीड़ इकट्ठा हो गई। ग्रिफिन उस जगह से दूर भाग गया। गली में किसी ने उसके पैर को कुचल दिया, उसके कंधे में भी एक खरोंच लग गई थी और सबसे बड़ी बात यह थी कि वह नंगा था और इसलिए उसे जुकाम भी हो गया था।

ग्रिफिन का असहाय होना

ग्रिफिन की शुरूआती खुशी समाप्त हो चुकी थी और अब वह यह सोचकर परेशान हो रहा था कि वह इस उलझन से कैसे निकलेगा। वह स्वयं को बहुत असहाय महसूस कर रहा था और उसे रोना भी आ गया। तभी एक कुत्ते ने उसे सूँघना शुरू कर दिया। ग्रिफिन को लगा कि कुत्ता उसे सूँघकर पकड़ सकता है। ग्रिफिन को एक बार फिर से पकड़े जाने का डर सताने लगा और वह वहाँ से भाग गया।

पैरों के बिना पदचिह्नों का बनना

सामने से एक Procession (जुलूस) आ रहा था और ग्रिफिन को लगा कि वह इससे होकर नहीं जा पाएगा। हालाँकि, वह अपने घर से ज्यादा दूर नहीं जाना चाहता था। वह वहाँ से भागकर एक घर की सफेद सीढ़ियों पर चला गया और उसके कीचड़ के पैरों ने नई सफेद सीढ़ियों पर निशान बना दिए। हैं। दो छोटे बच्चों ने उसके पदचिह्न देख लिए थे ग्रिफिन पकड़े जाने के डर से अत्यधिक घबरा गया था, परंतु किसी तरह से वह उन्हें चकमा देने में सफल हुआ।

Dr Kemp's Nervousness

Griffin was narrating to Dr Kemp his first outing as an Invisible Man. He was hurt and bruised. He had caught a cold also. Griffin saw people running as it was a fire. It was his lodging burning. Only his three books and a cheque book remained which he had put at the post-office. Dr Kemp was nervously looking outside and asked him to continue.

डॉ केंप की घबराहट

ग्रिफिन डॉ केंप को अदृश्य होने के बाद, पहली बार बाहर आने की बातें बता रहा था। उसे चोट, और खरोंच लगी। उसे जुकाम भी हो गया था। ग्रिफिन ने लोगों को भागते हुए देखा, क्योंकि कहीं आग लगी थी। यह उसका घर था जो जल रहा था। केवल उसकी तीन किताबें और चेकबुक बची थीं, जिन्हें उसने डाकघर में रखा था। डॉ केंप घबराहट से बाहर देख रहे थे और उन्होंने ग्रिफिन को कहानी जारी रखने के लिए कहा।

Word Meaning

Stumbled – लड़खड़ाना
Impulse – आवेग
Astray – दूर से
Concussion – आघात लगना
Folly – गलती
Heeding – ध्यान रखना
Hansom – ताँगा
Slime – चिकनी मिट्टी
Intimation – संकेत देना
Scrape – खरोंच आना
Blare – शोर मचाना
Bawling – रोना
Rum – अजीब
Impeded – रोक देना
Clumsiness – बेढंगा
Startle – झटका लगना
Revel – किसी में आनंद लेना
Incontinently – इरादतन
Dodge – झाँसा देना
Plunged – छलांग लगाना
Bruised – खरोंच आना
Amenable – सहमत होना
Sallied – घूमना
Brute – नीच
Spur – उकसाना
Hymn – भजन
Portico – बरामदा

Important Questions

Questions based on the Plot of the Chapter

Q 1. Griffin was filled with joy as he had an extraordinary advantage. Elaborate.

एक विशेष लाभ की प्राप्ति से ग्रिफिन अत्यधिक प्रसन्न था। वर्णन करें।

अदृश्यता का प्रयोग सफल होना – ग्रिफिन का वह प्रयोग स्वयं पर कर लेना – ग्रिफिन का अदृश्य होना – अदृश्य होकर बाहर निकल जाना – किसी का ग्रिफिन को नहीं देख पाना – ग्रिफिन का खुश होना – उसकी खुशी कि उसे बेहिसाब आजादी मिल गई है – अपनी इस सफलता को विशेष लाभ के रूप में देखना – इस आजादी के लिए ही अपना प्रयोग करना।

Ans. A brilliant scientist made a brilliant breakthrough by devising the formula to be invisible. When he performed this activity upon himself, he too became invisible. Now, nobody could see him, nobody could feel him, but the most amazing benefit that he had with him was that he could enjoy the impunity in his life.

He could do what he wished and to attain that long cherished freedom, Griffin had put the best of his skills and resources into act. He had long been wishing for this moment to come and when the moment came in his life, there were no bounds to his joy.

He termed his success to be an extraordinary advantage and really it was so when normal persons became different from one's abilities.

He went out to enjoy this newly acquired freedom and see how people were not able to notice him and when he made a naughty act, there was no one to stop him.

He was enjoying it by himself. He thought in his mind how nice it would be to remain invisible from the world. That's why Griffin was so much happy ever.

Q 2. What was the reaction of the two little children when they saw footprints without feet?

जब दो बच्चों ने बिना पैरों के पदचिह्न देखे, तो उनकी प्रतिक्रिया क्या थी?

ग्रिफिन का अदृश्य होना – अदृश्य होकर बाहर निकलना – बाहर घूमना और एक जगह कीचड़ में उसका पैर चला जाना – उसकी वजह से पैरों के निशान बनना – दो बच्चों का निशान के पीछे जाना, क्योंकि पैर वाले का पता न होना – बच्चों का उस निशान के पीछे चलते रहना – ग्रिफिन का एक जगह खड़ा होना – किसी तरह बच्चों को चकमा देकर भाग जाना।

Ans. When Griffin was done with his experiment on the cat, he got surprising results. He got to know that the drug he had formulated would be able to change the body of a creature. He was very happy on this and then he decided to repeat the experiment on himself.

He did it and got the same result, but coupled with the extreme happiness with it. He had got freedom. He went out of his lodgings to enjoy freedom. He went on the roads and did so much of mischiefs. Sometimes he threw the basket of some and other times he did something else.

He was really enjoying it to the full. Suddenly, he stepped into mud and as his feet were soaked with mud so when he started to walk on the ground, there were footprints which were being made on the ground. Two children spotted the imprint and started to follow him.

They were surprised at it and they did not let their chase down and kept on with it. They were standing close to Griffin as he was on a staircase to be away from a heading procession that he wanted to avoid. Eventually, he gave a slip to the boys and made his way.

Q 3. Griffin's first outing as an invisible man was a complete disaster. Comment.

ग्रिफिन का अदृश्य आदमी के तौर पर पहली बार बाहर जाना एक संपूर्ण मुसीबत थी। वर्णन करें।

ग्रिफिन का अदृश्य होकर पहली बार बाहर घूमने जाना – बाहर जाना उसके लिए आसान न होना – उसे चलने में दिक्कतें आना – उसका लड़खड़ाकर गिरना – कुत्तों द्वारा ग्रिफिन का पीछा किया जाना – ग्रिफिन का परेशान हो जाना – उसके पैरों में कीचड़ लग जाना – बच्चों द्वारा उसके पैरों के निशान का पीछा करना – ग्रिफिन को ठंड लगना – इस प्रकार उसकी पहली अदृश्य यात्रा का मुसीबत बन जाना।

Ans. Griffin managed to get the breakthrough that he was awaiting since long. It was being an Invisible Man. When he became invisible, he went on a nice strall to enjoy the bestowed freedom.

He was on the seventh sky about his success. With the same zeal, he went out and when he had gone, it was not all the way a pleasing idea, but it was a complete disaster to him. To start with the disaster, he had clashed with a man who was coming his way with a basket on his head. The man was not in a position to understand all this.

Griffin was having problems in walking too on the road as it was a new experience to him. Many times Griffin had stumbled on the road. Another of the disaster was that Griffin got continuous sniffing from a dog on the road. Griffin wanted to get rid of the dog as it might create doubts in the minds of the people there.

He was also chased by two boys when we was creating footprints on the ground and Griffin was trying to stay away from it. Eventually, he was able to give them a slip. The most important in this list of disaster was his being stark naked and in the chilly weather, it was just unbearable to Griffin.

In the Emporium

Griffin Searches for Food and Shelter

It was January and Griffin was in an awful state. He had no home, food and clothes. He also could not tell his secret to anyone.

It was biting cold and the first thing on his mind was to find shelter from the snow. Then, Griffin had a brilliant idea. He entered Omniums, a huge establishment where almost everything was available.

At Peace after a Long Time

Griffin decided to rob the place for food, clothing and other necessary things after the store was closed. Near the toy department, he had a brilliant idea. He could fake an appearance by using false items. Finally, he went to sleep and was at peace after a long time. But he had nightmares that night.

Out in the Open Again

Unfortunately for him, he slept till late and the store opened. He was spotted. The workers ran after him.

Griffin tried to hide but somebody saw him. He resorted to hurting his pursuers and created a mess at the store. Finally, he had to take all his clothes off to go out of sight.

In the Emporium

ग्रिफिन का भोजन और आश्रय की तलाश करना

जनवरी का समय था और Griffin (ग्रिफिन) की हालत बहुत ही खराब थी। उसके पास घर, खाना और कपड़े नहीं थे। वह अपना राज भी किसी को नहीं बता सकता था।

सर्दी अपने रोष पर थी और उसके दिमाग में पहली बात, बर्फ से बचने के लिए आश्रय ढूढ़ँना थी। तभी ग्रिफिन को एक बेहतरीन विचार आया। वह Omniums (ओमनियम्स) में दाखिल हुआ जोकि एक बड़ा भवन था और उसमें जरूरत की लगभग सभी चीजें मौजूद थी।

लंबे समय के बाद सुकून मिलना

ग्रिफिन ने स्टोर बंद हो जाने के बाद उसमें से भोजन, कपड़े और अन्य जरूरत की चीजें चुराने का फैसला किया। खिलौनों के स्टोर पर जाने के बाद उसके दिमाग में एक बेहतरीन विचार आया। वह नकली चीजों के साथ अपना चेहरा बदल सकता था। अंतत: वह सोने के लिए चला गया और लंबे समय के बाद उसे सुकून का अहसास हो रहा था। परंतु उस रात उसे बुरे सपने आए थे।

खुले में फिर से बाहर आना

दुर्भाग्यवश वह देर तक सोता रहा और स्टोर खुल चुका था। उसे पकड़ लिया गया था। काम करने वाले उसके पीछे भागे।

ग्रिफिन ने छिपने की कोशिश की, परंतु किसी ने उसे देख लिया था। पीछा करने वालों को उसने पीटा और पूरे स्टोर में अफरा-तफरी मचा दी। अंतत: उसने उस जगह से बाहर निकलने के लिए अपने सारे कपड़े उतार दिए थे।

Word Meaning

Wretched	– दुःखी	Confide	– राज रखना
Rarity	– दुर्लभता	Accost	– संबोधित करना
Evoke	– ताजा करना	Latched	– सिटकनी लगा होना
Impregnably	– जिसे जीता न जा सके	Meandering	– फैला हुआ होना
Personage	– मान्य व्यक्ति	Contrived	– योजना बनाना
Wicker	– लचीली	Prowled	– शिकार की खोज करना
Bedsteads	– चारपाई	Flock	– ऊन
Vociferating	– गुस्से में जोर से चिल्लाना	Procure	– प्राप्त करना
Alacrity	– जीवांत होना	Lair	– छिपने की जगह
Festoons	– सजावट	Receptacles	– सामान रखने का डिब्बा
Swathed	– पट्टी लगाना	Intricate	– छोटी-छोटी चीजें

Important Questions

Questions based on the Plot of the Chapter

Q 1. Why did Griffin decide to seek shelter urgently?

ग्रिफिन को तुरंत आश्रय की आवश्यकता क्यों पड़ी?

ग्रिफिन का अदृश्यता का प्रयोग सफल होना – अदृश्य होकर उसका बेहद खुश होना – अपनी नई-नई आजादी को भुनाने के लिए उसका बाहर निकलना – बाहर उसका कई समस्याओं से सामना होना – जबरदस्त सर्दी झेलना – कुत्तों द्वारा परेशान किया जाना – चलने में भी कष्ट होना – अतः ग्रिफिन का अपने लिए आश्रय की तलाश करना।

Ans. Griffin had successfully completed his experiment and he became invisible. It was a pleasurable moment for him. He had long been wishing for this dream to come true. Being invisible meant a great impunity for him. He went out to have the pleasure of this impunity. As he went out, he realised that there were lots of drawbacks of being invisible.

He was unable to walk properly as he was staggering on the road. When he thought of a vehicle coming from the front and to take a side he was not, there were a lot of problems. His feet were damp with falling snow on the ground and he was finding it very difficult to walk.

He was also a constant victim of sniffing dogs that were able to recognise him then.

He was stark naked and he was feeling the impulse of coldness in him. He then, felt the need of a shelter and got to know the instant importance of it.

Had he not been able to get a shelter soon then he might have been a man frosted with all his muscles and bones. That's why Griffin decided to have any kind of shelter for him just that moment, so that he could survive the fury of cold.

Q 2. What made Griffin go to the huge departmental store? Why he had to wait till the store was empty?

ग्रिफिन एक बड़े स्टोर में क्यों गया था? स्टोर के खाली होने तक वह बाहर इंतजार क्यों करता रहा?

अदृश्यता का लाभ लेने के लिए ग्रिफिन का बाहर जाना – उसे बाहर की कठिनाइयों का पता चलना – कुत्तों का उसका पीछा करना – सर्दी के अहसास के बाद आश्रय की जरूरत – उसका एक स्टोर की तरफ जाना – स्टोर में हर चीज की उपलब्धता होना – स्टोर में कर्मचारियों व ग्राहकों का होना – ग्रिफिन का बाहर इंतजार करना कि सारे लोग जाएँ, ताकि वह अपने तरीके से काम कर सके और लाभ उठा सके।

Ans. When Griffin set out for enjoying his freedom that he had got from being invisible, all his experiences were bad. He felt awkward to walk on the ground.

He was even chased by a few dogs. He was feeling the strong impulse of the cold outside and it became more and more with his being stark naked. He knew at once that he was in need of a shelter very soon.

His own rented shelter had been burnt by him and he could not go there as a consequence. He had made no friends as he wanted to keep all his work a secret. The problem was just surmounting and he was still to find answers. That's when he was struck with a brilliant piece of an idea.

He thought of going to a big departmental store where he would be able to find food, clothes and shelter everyting under one single roof. So, he reached the store soon. The store was full with the workers and the customers who were there to shop. Griffin had to wait till all the customers and workers leave the premise for the day. When the store would be empty, Griffin would be having the best of his chances to do what he wished.

In Drury Lane

Griffin was at a Disadvantage

Griffin continued with his story and told Dr Kemp that he was at a disadvantage due to his condition as he could not eat, had no shelter, no clothes and it was snowing. Even the rain and fog could give away his secret.

Griffin's Plan

Griffin was immediately struck by an idea. He decided to cover his face with a mask and a wig. He began his search for a theatrical costumiers shop where he could get the desired costume.

Finally, Griffin reached the object of his quest. It was an old-fashioned shop with a four storey house above it. There was no one in the shop. The gate had a bell and immediately the owner of the house, a short hunchbacked man, came running down.

The Man had a Very Sharp Hearing

He was a vigilant and alert person with an acute sense of hearing. The man was washing his plates when Griffin put some coal in the fire. Immediately, the man came running upstairs.

Griffin was angry but decided to put on some clothes, but in the process, a pile from the upper shelf fell. The short man came and actually touched Griffin. He was amazed but then thought that it was rats.

In Drury Lane

ग्रिफिन को लाभ न होना

Griffin (ग्रिफिन) Dr Kemp (डॉ. कैंप) को अपनी कहानी सुना रहा था और उसने यह बताया कि उस समय असुविधा के कारण उसकी स्थिति ठीक नहीं थी क्योंकि वह खा नहीं सकता था, उसके पास घर व कपड़े भी नहीं थे और बर्फबारी भी हो रही थी। यहाँ तक कि बारिश और धुंध भी उसकी अदृश्यता का राज खोल सकते थे।

ग्रिफिन की योजना

ग्रिफिन के दिमाग में तुरंत एक विचार आया। उसने अपने चेहरे को मुखौटे और विग से ढकने का निश्चय किया। उसने Theatrical Costumiers (रंगमंच की ड्रेस) वाली दुकान के लिए खोज शुरू कर दी, जिसमें से वह मनचाही ड्रेस ले सकें।

अंततः ग्रिफिन अपनी तलाश वाली दुकान तक पहुँच गया। यह एक पुरानी दुकान थी, जिसके ऊपर चार मंजिला मकान भी बना हुआ था। दुकान के अंदर कोई भी नहीं था। दरवाजे पर एक घंटी भी लगी हुई थी और जल्दी से घर का मालिक वहाँ पर भाग कर आया, जो एक कम कूबड़ वाला व्यक्ति था।

आदमी की सुनने की क्षमता का बहुत तेज होना

वह Vigilant (चौकन्ना) और सतर्क व्यक्ति था, जिसकी सुनने की शक्ति बहुत तेज थी। वह आदमी अपनी प्लेट धो रहा था जब ग्रिफिन ने आग में कुछ कोयले ड़ालें। वह आदमी तुरंत भागता हुआ ऊपर आया।

ग्रिफिन बहुत गुस्से में था परंतु वह कुछ कपड़े पहन लेना चाहता था, कपड़े उतारने की प्रकिया में ऊपरी तह पर रखे हुए कुछ कपड़े उसके ऊपर गिर पड़े। छोटा आदमी अंदर आया और उसने ग्रिफिन को वास्तव में छुआ। उसे आश्चर्य हुआ परंतु उसे लगा कि वह चूहा होगा।

Griffin Finds Many Things

Now Griffin was alone in the house. He began his search. Firstly, he went for the food, which he found in the storeroom. He also found some make-up material. He also found some masks, glasses and other stuff. There was money also. After getting dressed up, he was not sure and checked his appearance thoroughly till he was convinced that he can pull it off.

ग्रिफिन को अनेक चीजें मिलना

अब ग्रिफिन घर में अकेला था। उसने अपनी खोज शुरू की। पहले उसने खाना खोजा, जो उसे भंडार-घर में मिल गया। उसे मेकअप का कुछ सामान भी मिला। उसे कुछ मुखौटे, चश्मे और अन्य सामान मिला। उसे कुछ पैसे भी मिले। कपड़े पहनने के पश्चात् उसे संतुष्टि नहीं हुई और उसने अपने आपको तब तक आईने में देखा जब तक कि उसे पूर्ण संतुष्टि नहीं हो गई।

Griffin Troubles were not Over

Griffin grew over-confident only to realise that he could even eat out in the open. He found himself in a private room saying that he was badly disfigured. He had never dreamt of so many troubles that would encounter him after getting invisible. He was trying to get visible again.

ग्रिफिन की समस्याओं का अंत नहीं

ग्रिफिन को जरूरत से ज्यादा विश्वास हो गया था और उसे लग रहा था कि वह अब बाहर जाकर खाना भी खा सकेगा। वह एक निजी कमरे में जाकर बैठा और उसने बताया कि उसका चेहरा थोड़ा बदनुमा हो गया है। उसने कभी सोचा भी न था कि जब वह अदृश्य हो जाएगा तो उसे इतनी सारी परेशानियों का सामना करना पड़ेगा। वह पुनः दृश्य होने का प्रयास कर रहा था।

Word Meaning

Grotesquely – विकृत रूप से
Tomfoolery – बेवकूफी से भरा
Tinsel – चमकदार
Dominoes – नुकीले कपड़े
Clanking – झनझनाहट
Beetle-browed – घनी भौंहें
Scullery – बर्तन धोने की जगह
Ace – एक ईंच
Smuts – धूल
Array – कतार
Sham – नकली
Dismal – निराशा
Rummage – छानबीन करना
Muttering – बड़बड़ाना
Aglare – आँखें फाड़ कर देखना
Plank – लकड़ी का तख्ता

Infernal	– बहुत परेशान करने वाला	Conventions	– व्यवहार
Gagged	– प्रतिबंध लगाना	Render	– रूपांतरित करना
Calico	– एक प्रकार का कपड़ा	Appetite	– भूख की ईच्छा
Absurdity	– फूहड़पन	Philanthropy	– मानवीय
Caricature	– प्रतिरूपण	Roving	– आवारगी

Important Questions

Questions based on the Plot of the Chapter

Q 1. What was Griffin's plan when he realised that he was at a disadvantage?

जब ग्रिफिन को उसकी कमियों का पता चला तो उसने क्या योजना बनाई थी?

ग्रिफिन का लंबे समय के बाद शोध में सफल होना – ग्रिफिन का अदृश्य होना – उसे अदृश्यता की कमियों के बारे में पता चलना – लोगों से संपर्क न हो पाना – उसकी योजना कि वह दुबारा से दृश्य होगा – इसके लिए उसकी नकली नाक, मूँछें, बाल आदि लगाने की सोच होना – उसका इन सामानों के लिए डूरी लेन की तरफ जाना – लोगों के लिए उसका एक कहानी बनाना कि एक हादसे में उसका चेहरा बदनुमा हो गया है।

Ans. After the long-term of the experiment, Griffin got the blessed result. He was a man who was invisible then. He had always wished to be such a man who could be seen by none. He had imagined that it was a boon to be invisible. Now, when he was invisible, he got to realise that there are many disadvantages alongwith it. He had faced such disadvantages. He was chased by dogs. He faced the difficulty in walking too. He had to contend with the persons, who were following him. In a way, the disadvantages were enough and he was faded up. So, he planned to make a way out of it. He decided to become a visible man.

If not completely then partially. He thought and thought for long and came to a conclusion that if he could manage to get a false nose, whiskers and wigs, matter could be exciting. He moved towards the Drury Lane where there were a lot of shops which offered the stuffs for sale suitable to Griffin. His intention was to get those outfits and then to make himself a partially visible man. He had a story in his mind that he would say people that an accident had disfigured his face that way. This was his plan for the next phase.

Q 2. Griffin thought that as an invisible, he could easily rob anyone. However, the hunchback made it a hard task. Elaborate.

ग्रिफिन ने सोचा कि अपनी अदृश्यता का लाभ लेकर वह किसी को भी आसानी से लूट सकेगा। परंतु उस कुबड़े आदमी ने उसका यह काम मुश्किल कर दिया था। वर्णन करें।

ग्रिफिन का सोचना कि अदृश्य होने पर लाभ होना– अवसरों पर ग्रिफिन द्वारा फायदा उठाना–ग्रिफिन का ड्रूरी लेन की एक दुकान में चोरी करना– दुकान के मालिक का कुबड़ा मनुष्य होना– उसकी सुनने की क्षमता का तेज होना– चूहे का अहसास होना– उसे पता चलना कि दुकान के अंदर कोई है–दुकान बंद करना और तुरंत वापस आना–चोरी के लिए ग्रिफिन का उसको मार कर लिटा देना।

Ans. Being invisible could be a great advantage in many cases, but for Griffin the same couldn't be thought. Griffin had thought that if he could be invisible, he would have an edge in the coming phase of his life. He would be able to do whatever he wished and he would be able to rob anyone without getting noticed even. At few times, it was so when he robbed someone and did not get noticed. With the same spirit, he entered a theatrical shop in the Drury Lane where he was supposed to get the theatrical accoutrements. The owner was a hunchbacked man.

When Griffin entered his shop, the owner was out of the shop for a while. Griffin was busy with analysing the stuffs that he needed for the purpose. As the stuffs tumbled a bit, the man entered with the sound and got surprised seeing no one inside. He took the sound to be of a rat.

Griffin waited for a moment and again started his due movement, but the hunchbacked man was so attentive that he realised the presence of a figure in his shop. He was just sure about that but again taking his doubt, he closed the door and went out. He entered again hearing some sound. Finally, Griffin had to hit him down to rob him.

Question based on the Character Sketch

Q 1. Attempt a character-sketch of the hunchbacked man?

कुबड़े मनुष्य का चरित्र-चित्रण करें।

कुबड़े मनुष्य ड्रूरी लेन में दुकान चलाता था – उसकी सुनने की क्षमता बहुत तेज होना – ग्रिफिन का उसकी दुकान में चोरी करने के लिए घुसना – कुबड़े मनुष्य का आहट सुनते ही आ जाना। – ग्रिफिन को चोरी करने में दिक्कतें पैदा करना– चौकन्ना तथा सजग होना – अन्त में ग्रिफिन द्वारा उसकों मार कर बेहोश करना।

Ans. The hunchbacked man bad a costume hop in the Drury Lane. When Griffin was in search of a suitable costume that could cover him and he might be visible partially than he ran into the shop of the hunchbacked man.

A the moment of Griffin's entry he was out of his hop but entered there just after a slight sound was produce by Griffin. As he entered his shop he was certain that somebody was at work there. He became so alert that it became difficult for Griffin to have his next move.

The hunchbacked was very keen and he started to search the scrumptious movement. Griffin had idea that he should leave the place and as he was on the stair case he was still under watch ful eyes. Griffin had to knock him down and then set on the robbery. This revealed that the hunchbacked man had got a fighting spirit with him.

The Plan that Failed

Griffin Continues with his Story

Dr Kemp saw some men coming up to the house and he tried to keep Griffin busy. He asked about Griffin's plans. Griffin said that he was trying to get out of the country to a much warmer place.

It would not have been difficult for an Invisible Man. But Mr Marvel ran away with his books and money. The books were vital and he wanted them back.

Griffin's Sinister Plans

Griffin said that meeting with Dr Kemp has changed his plans. He is now thinking of all the things that he can manage to do with the help of Dr Kemp. He further talks of the purposes for which he can use his invisibility. Finally Griffin confides in Dr Kemp his plan to establish a reign of terror. To do this, he wanted to murder someone. Dr Kemp is shocked and tries to tell him otherwise. But Griffin wanted to kill all those who come in his way.

Dr Kemp has Cheated Griffin

Just then, sounds were heard from downstairs. Dr Kemp knew that it was the police and he tried to divide Griffin's attention. But when Griffin tried to open the door, Dr Kemp blocked him. In an instant, Griffin realised that Dr Kemp had cheated him. He takes his clothes off, hits Dr Kemp as hard as he could and before anyone could make a move, he had escaped.

The Plan that Failed

ग्रिफिन का अपनी कहानी के जारी रखना

Dr Kemp (डॉ कैंप) ने घर की तरफ कुछ लोगों को आते हुए देखा इसलिए उन्होंने Griffin (ग्रिफिन) को व्यस्त रखने की कोशिश की। उन्होंने ग्रिफिन की आगे की योजना के बारे में पूछा। ग्रिफिन ने बताया कि वह एक ऐसे देश में जाना चाहता था जहाँ गर्मी थोड़ी ज्यादा हो।

यह एक Invisible Man (अदृश्य आदमी) के लिए मुश्किल नहीं होता। लेकिन Mr Marvel (मि मार्वेल) उसकी किताबें और धन लेकर भाग गया था। किताबें महत्त्वपूर्ण थी और वह उन्हें वापस चाहता था।

ग्रिफिन की खतरनाक योजनाएँ

ग्रिफिन ने कहा कि डॉ कैंप से मिलने के बाद उसकी सारी Plans (योजनाएँ) बदल चुकी हैं। अब वह उन सारी चीजों के बारे में सोच रहा था, जिन्हें वह डॉ कैंप की सहायता से कर सकता था। अंततः उसने अदृश्यता से मिलने वाले लाभ के बारे में भी बताया था। ग्रिफिन ने डॉ कैंप को भरोसेमंद मानते हुए A Reign of Terror (आतंक का राज कायम) करने की अपनी योजना के बारे में बताया। ऐसा करने के लिए वह किसी की हत्या करना चाहता था। डॉ कैंप को यह सुनकर आश्चर्य हुआ और उन्होंने उसे अन्य तरह से समझाने की कोशिश की। परंतु ग्रिफिन अपने मार्ग में आने वाले प्रत्येक व्यक्ति को मार देना चाहता था।

डॉ कैंप का ग्रिफिन को धोखा देना

इस बीच नीचे कुछ आवाजें सुनाई दीं। डॉ कैंप समझ गए कि वे पुलिस के लोग हैं और उन्होंने ग्रिफिन का ध्यान बँटाने की कोशिश की लेकिन जब ग्रिफिन ने दरवाजा खोलने की कोशिश की, तो डॉ कैंप ने उसे रोका। एक क्षण में ही ग्रिफिन समझ गया कि डॉ कैंप ने उसे धोखा दिया है। ग्रिफिन ने अपने सारे कपड़े उतारे और डॉ कैंप के सिर पर जोर से प्रहार किया और इससे पहले कि कोई कुछ करता, वह वहाँ से भाग निकला।

Word Meaning

Altered	– बदलना	Vague	– दिखावा
Wanton	– बिना उद्‌देश्य के	Eavesdropping	– जासूसी करना
Slaying	– कत्ल करना	Confederate	– साथी
Traitor	– धोखेबाज	Wedging	– फँसाना
Pitched	– फेंक देना	Aghast	– यकीन न कर पाना

Important Questions

Questions based on the Plot of the Chapter

Q 1. What was Dr Kemp trying to hide from Griffin? Why did Griffin call him a traitor?

डॉ केंप ग्रिफिन से क्या छिपाने की कोशिश कर रहे थे? ग्रिफिन ने उनको धोखेबाज क्यों कहा?

ग्रिफिन का डॉ केंप के घर में छिपना – उनके घर खाना व आराम करना – डॉ केंप के द्वारा कर्नल एडी को नोट लिखना – डॉ केंप का चुपके से ही पुलिस को बुलाना – पदचाप सुनाई देना – पुलिस के आने पर ग्रिफिन का ध्यान भटकाना – ग्रिफिन का समझना कि पुलिस डॉ केंप के इशारे पर आई है – डॉ केंप द्वारा ग्रिफिन को धोखा देना – ग्रिफिन का अपनी योजना डॉ केंप को भी बताना – ग्रिफिन द्वारा डॉ केंप को धोखेबाज कहना।

Ans. Griffin took shelter in the house of Dr Kemp who was his college mate. Griffin was given food, cloth and shelter by Dr Kemp. Griffin slept the whole night while Dr Kemp was busy with getting details about Griffin from the newspaper. When he got all the details, he wrote a note to Colonel Adye about Griffin. The very next morning, Colonel Adye alongwith his fellows came to the house of Dr Kemp. The sounds of the footsteps were clearly heard from the distance even. Dr Kemp tried to divide attention of Griffin so that the policemen may work smoothly.

As Griffin got up to enquire about the sound, he was then blocked by Dr Kemp. Griffin understood that something wrong was going to take place. He got the idea that Dr Kemp had cheated him and he was responsible for the police's arrival to the house. He had confided in Dr Kemp but the latter had cheated him. That's why Dr Kemp was called to be a traitor by Griffin. Dr Kemp was hiding the fact of the arrival of Colonel Adye to the house from Griffin at his best level.

Q 2. Justify the title of the chapter, 'The Plan that Failed'.

पाठ के शीर्षक 'The Plan that Failed' को सत्यापित करें।

अदृश्य ग्रिफिन का डॉ केंप के घर जाना – डॉ केंप द्वारा उसे भोजन, कपड़ा व आश्रय देना – अगली सुबह ग्रिफिन का डॉ केंप को अपनी सारी योजना बताना – पहली योजना उसकी एक गर्मी वाले देश में जाने की – डॉ केंप से मिलने के बाद योजना बदल लेना – नई योजना के अनुसार उसका और डॉ केंप का बरडॉक में आतंक का राज कायम करना – खून व हत्याएँ होनी – डॉ केंप के द्वारा पुलिस को बुलाना – ग्रिफिन को धोखा देना – योजना का क्रियान्वयन न हो पाना – पाठ का शीर्षक तर्कसंगत।

Ans. Brilliant scientist Griffin had managed to be an Invisible Man. He had planned this for a long time and when this turned out to be a reality, happiness is due and worth. He had thought that being invisible would give him a lot of freedom to enjoy, but consequences were not optimal. When all these were happening, Griffin run into Dr Kemp, his college mate. He spent time with him and Dr Kemp had provided him with shelter, food and clothes. Dr Kemp also gave him his words that he would conceal his presence in the house.

Next day, Griffin laid out all his plans before Dr Kemp. At first, Griffin wanted to shift to a country that should be warm enough to adjust with Griffin's invisibility. But, after meeting with Dr Kemp, Griffin changed all his plans altogether. Now, he wished to create a reign of terror at the Burdock Port by committing a murder.

He decided to kill all who comes ever in his way even by chance. All these plans were to be executed with the help of Dr Kemp, but he cheated Griffin by calling the police and as a consequence, all the plans failed. Hence, the title of the chapter is well justified.

The Hunting of the Invisible Man

Griffin is Pure Selfishness

Dr Kemp could hardly speak after his fight with Griffin. Dr Kemp told police that Griffin was mad. He was a selfish human being. He further said that Griffin must be stopped or he will next turn to kill people as he want to create panic.

The Plan was Set

Dr Kemp said that every available man should be put to hunt. He wanted to stop Griffin from escaping. Dr Kemp knew that the only thing that could stop him from leaving the place was his three books. Colonel Adye informed him that Mr Marvel denies having those books. Dr Kemp said that they must stop him from eating or sleeping and every single person should be on alert.

Griffin is Responsible for his Bad Consequences

Dr Kemp further said that they should use dogs as they could smell him. Colonel Adye said that he could arrange for bloodhounds. Another important thing was that the food eaten by Griffin was visible until it had been absorbed. Dr Kemp also wanted powdered glass on the roads as Griffin was bare feet. Dr Kemp feared that he would now be more furious, but Griffin was the one who had gone against humanity and whatever happened to him, only he was responsible for the bad consequences.

The Hunting of the Invisible Man

ग्रिफिन का पूर्णरूप से स्वार्थी होना

Griffin (ग्रिफिन) से लड़ने के बाद Dr Kemp (डॉ केंप) शायद ही बोल पा रहे थे। डॉ केंप ने पुलिस को बताया कि ग्रिफिन पागल हो चुका है। वह एक स्वार्थी मनुष्य हो चुका था। उन्होंने यह भी बताया कि यदि ग्रिफिन को नहीं रोका गया, तो वह आतंक फैलाने के लिए लोगों को मारना शुरू कर देगा।

योजना बनाना

डॉ केंप ने कहा कि प्रत्येक आदमी को हमला करने के लिए तैयार रहना चाहिए। वे ग्रिफिन को भागने से रोकना चाहते थे। डॉ केंप जानते थे कि केवल उसकी तीन किताबें ही उसे वह स्थान छोड़ने से रोक सकती हैं। Colonel Adye (कर्नल एडी) ने बताया कि Mr Marvel (मि मार्वेल) उन किताबों के लिए इंकार कर रहा है। डॉ केंप ने कहा, उसे खाना खाने व सोने से रोकना होगा और प्रत्येक व्यक्ति को सावधान रहना होगा।

अपनी दुर्दशा के लिए ग्रिफिन का स्वयं जिम्मेदार होना

डॉ केंप ने कहा कि कुत्ते उसे सूँघकर पहचान सकते हैं अत: कुत्तों को काम पर लगा सकते हैं। कर्नल एडी ने कहा कि वे Bloodhounds (खोजी कुत्तों) का प्रबंध कर सकते हैं। उन्हें यह भी बताया गया कि ग्रिफिन के द्वारा खाया गया भोजन जब तक पचता नहीं है तब तक वह दिखाई देता है। डॉ केंप ने रास्तों पर Powdered Glass (काँच का चूरा) बिछाने को कहा, जिससे ग्रिफिन के Bare Feet (नंगे पैर) जख्मी हो जाएँ। डॉ केंप का मानना था कि ग्रिफिन अब और भी खतरनाक हो जाएगा, परंतु वह अकेला था, जो मानवता के विरुद्ध गया था और इस दुर्दशा के लिए वह स्वयं जिम्मेदार था।

Word Meaning

Inarticulate	– उलझन में होना	Maiming	– किसी को चोट पहुँचाना
Garrison	– पुलिस के जवान	Astir	– जीवंत रहना
Bloodhounds	– कुत्तों की नस्ल	Assimilated	– अवशोषित होना
Establish	– स्थापना करना	Inkling	– आभास होना
Haste	– जल्दीबाजी	Striding	– लंबे डग भरना
Customary	– परंपरागत	Witch Craft	– काला जादू
Gentry	– उच्च वर्गीय लोग	Apprentice	– नवसिखुआ
Asserted	– बरकरार रखना	Accord	– इच्छा
Amazement	– आश्चर्य	Viciously	– बुरे तरीके से
Tremendous	– बहुत ज्यादा	Terminated	– समाप्ति होना

Important Questions

Questions based on the Plot of the Chapter

Q 1. What elaborate plans were made to catch Griffin?
ग्रिफिन को पकड़ने के लिए क्या योजनाएँ बनाई गई थीं?

ग्रिफिन का अपना राज डॉ केंप को बताना – ग्रिफिन पर पुलिस का खतरा – ग्रिफिन का भाग जाना – डॉ केंप का उसको पकड़ने की योजना बनाना – उनका कर्नल एडी को सलाह देना – तीन महत्त्वपूर्ण किताबों के न मिल जाने तक गाँव को न छोड़ना – उसे खाना खाने व आराम करने से रोकना – उसे कुत्तों द्वारा पकड़ने की योजना बनाना – रास्तों पर काँच का चूर्ण बिछा देना – उसके नंगे पैरों में काँच चुभने के बाद उसे पकड़ना – सारी योजनाएँ ग्रिफिन के खिलाफ डॉ केंप के द्वारा बनाई जानी।

Ans. Griffin had told all his secrets to Dr Kemp. What were his plans, what were his intentions and all that were known to Griffin had been disclosed before Dr Kemp. On the same concern Dr Kemp told all these to police and then there were execution of plans to catch Griffin.

All these plans were made by Dr Kemp. He suggested to Colonel Adye that he would not leave the town until he gets his three valuable books. When Dr Kemp came to know that Mr Marvel had not those three books, he told that Griffin must not be allowed to eat anything as food would force him to break in.

Also, if he managed to get food, he must not be allowed to take rest because the unassimilated food remains visible in him. Next idea was to call the dogs as he could be sniffed by the dogs and might be caught. Another plan was to put the powdered glass into the roads and when Griffin would walk barefoot over the glass, his feet would bleed and he would be caught easily by the police. All these plans were made by Dr Kemp and he knew that he could be well able to catch Griffin by any of the means above.

Question based on the Character Sketch

Q 2. What impression does Dr Kemp leave on you?

डॉ केंप के बारे में आपकी क्या राय है?

डॉ केंप का एक प्रखर वैज्ञानिक का होना – समाज की भलाई चाहना – उनका ग्रिफिन के नापाक इरादों को कामयाब होने से रोकना – उनका चुपके से पुलिस को बुलाना – पुलिस को ग्रिफिन को पकड़ने में मदद करना – डॉ केंप की एक बेहतरीन योजना बनाना – उनकी योजना को ही ध्यान में रखते हुए पुलिस का ग्रिफिन के लिए जाल बिछाना – लोगों द्वारा डॉ केंप की बात का यकीन करना और उनकी बुद्धिमत्ता पर सबको यकीन होना।

Ans. He was a true brilliancy in the field of science. When Griffin revealed all the secrets before Dr Kemp, he latter realised that Griffin's intention was not good at all. He was trying to harm the society and its elements. Dr Kemp decided to object Griffin in his ill-will. He wrote a note to Colonel Adye so that he might be able to get the man easily. This shows that Kemp had a prosociety approach and he had a strong bond with the society. Next, Dr Kemp was a meticulous planner.

He planned well to gain confidence of Griffin and then took all the secrets out of him. After doing this all, he secretly sent for the police. When his mate made his escape, Kemp came out with good ideas to catch-up with Griffin.

He directed the policemen so that they could be able to get Griffin soon. He advised them to prevent him from taking three valuable books. Also, he told them to restrict him from eating and resting. Roads were sprinkled with glass powder on his words. This tells us that his words were believed to be true.

The Wicksteed Murder

Griffin is Filled with Rage

The narrator continues by giving the details of Griffin's ferocious nature. He was filled with rage when he ran from Dr Kemp's house and he threw a little child so hard that his ankle was broken. After that, his trace for hours. But the narrator says that one can imagine his state of mind.

Griffin is Hurt by Dr Kemp's Treachery

The narrator says that there was no doubt in Griffin being hurt and highly irritated by what had Dr Kemp done with him. After two o'clock, it would have become difficult to escape using trains and the whole town was on high alert.

In the evening, he must have read the proclamations, saw the doors locked and must have realised that the information he gave to Dr Kemp is being used against him.

Mr Wicksteed is Murdered

Before nightfall, the town was filled with terror as the news of Mr Wicksteed's murder spread. The narrator is not sure about the events that led to his brutal death, but everyone suspected that it was Griffin who had done it.

Mr Wicksteed was last seen alive by a little girl. Mr Wicksteed was beaten by an iron rod. The evidences showed that the Invisible Man was at work.

The Wicksteed Murder

ग्रिफिन का गुस्से से भरा होना

कथाकार ने Griffin (ग्रिफिन) के गुस्से वाले रवैये की कहानी जारी रखी। जब वह Dr Kemp (डॉ केंप) के घर से बाहर निकला, तो बहुत ज्यादा गुस्से में था और उसने एक छोटे बच्चे को इतने जोर से पटका कि उसका पैर टूट गया। इसके बाद, घंटों तक उसका कोई पता नहीं था। परंतु कथाकार ने कहा कि उसकी मानसिक अवस्था का अंदाजा लगाया जा सकता था।

ग्रिफिन को डॉ केंप की धोखेबाजी से आघात पहुँचना

The Narrator (कथाकार) ने बताया कि इसमें कोई शक नहीं था कि डॉ केंप ने ग्रिफिन के साथ जो कुछ भी किया, उससे उसे आघात पहुँचा। दो बजे के बाद ट्रेनों का प्रयोग करके वहाँ से निकलना और दुष्कर हो गया था, और पूरा शहर सावधान था।

शाम तक ग्रिफिन को अपने खिलाफ चल रहे अभियान की जानकारी हो चुकी थी, उसने घरों के दरवाजे बंद देखे और वह समझ गया कि डॉ केंप को दी गई सारी जानकारी अब उसके खिलाफ इस्तेमाल हो रही थी।

मि विकस्टीड की हत्या हो जाना

रात होने से पहले पूरा शहर दहशत में आ गया था क्योंकि Mr Wicksteed (मि विकस्टीड) की हत्या की खबर फैल चुकी थी। कथाकार को हत्या के कारणों का पक्का पता नहीं था, परंतु लोग यही शक कर रहे थे कि यह ग्रिफिन ही होगा, जिसने यह किया हैं।

मि विकस्टीड को आखिरी बार जिंदा एक छोटी लड़की ने देखा था। मि विकस्टीड को लोहे के डंडे से मारा गया था। इन घटनाओं से स्पष्ट हो गया था कि अदृश्य आदमी अपनी हरकतों को जारी रखे हुए था।

The Invisible Man's Remorse

The narrator again states that Griffin could have avoided the man, but in the position he was or was put by the residents of the town forced him to commit the murder, though it is pure hypothesis. The narrator thinks that the sight of Mr Wicksteed lying in blood must have filled Griffin with remorse. But he was being hunt and this made him struggle. The next day, he was ready to prepare for a fight back.

अदृश्य आदमी का पश्चाताप

कथाकार पुनः कहता है कि ग्रिफिन उस व्यक्ति को छोड़ सकता था, परंतु जिस स्थिति में वह था या जो स्थिति गाँव के लोगों ने पैदा की थी, उन्होंने उसे हत्या करने पर मजबूर किया था, यद्यपि ये सारी घटनाएँ काल्पनिकता के कारणों से भरी पड़ी थीं। कथाकार ने माना कि मि विकस्टीड को खून से लथपथ जमीन पर पड़ा देखकर ग्रिफिन को पश्चाताप जरूर हुआ होगा। लेकिन लोग उसके पीछे थे और इस वजह से वह झल्लाया हुआ था। अगले दिन भी वह एक लड़ाई के लिए तैयार था।

Word Meaning

Perceptions – अवधारणा
Ecstatically – खुशी से
Deceit – धोखा
Ken – जानकारी
Antagonist – शत्रु
Incessant – लगातार
Siege – घेराबंदी
Trampled – कुचला हुआ
Frenzy – पागलपन
Provoke – उकसाना
Trotting – धीरे-धीरे चलना
Clump – भीड़-झुंड
Quarry – खदान
Egotistical – अहंकारी
Remorse – पछतावा
Wailing – कष्ट
Shattered – ध्वस्त करना
Treachery – धोखेबाजी
Brutal – क्रूर
Proclamation – घोषणा करना
Bludgeons – डंडा
Stringent – सख्त
Sallied – जोखिमपूर्ण कदम
Splintered – टुकड़े-टुकड़े करना
Inoffensive – हानि न पहुँचाने वाला
Feeble – कमजोर
Pantomime – नकल करना
Inexplicably – रहस्यात्मक रूप से
Irascibility – खीझ पैदा करने वाला
Pent – रचनाएँ
contrived – अवास्तविक
Clover – घास

Important Questions

Questions based on Plot of the Chapter

Q 1. Mr Wicksteed was a victim of circumstances. Comment.

मि विकस्टीड परिस्थितियों के शिकार हो गए थे। वर्णन करें।

ग्रिफिन का डॉ केंप के घर में रुकना – डॉ केंप के द्वारा खाना, कपड़े और रहने की सुविधाएँ देना – डॉ केंप के द्वारा किसी को न बताने की जबान देना – ग्रिफिन का सारी योजनाएँ डॉ केंप को बताना – कर्नल एडी को पत्र लिखना – डॉ केंप का ग्रिफिन को धोखा देना – ग्रिफिन का किसी तरह डॉ केंप के घर से निकलना – ग्रिफिन का गुस्से में होना – रास्ते में मि विकस्टीड का आ जाना – ग्रिफिन के लिए उसके मन में कोई गलत इरादा न होना – ग्रिफिन द्वारा मि विकस्टीड के सिर पर लोहे के डंडे से प्रहार करना – मि विकस्टीड का बिना वजह मारा जाना – अतः कहा जा सकता है कि परिस्थितियों की वजह से उसकी हत्या हो गई।

Ans. When Griffin had a stay at the house of Dr Kemp then he was provided with food, clothes and shelter. Dr Kemp gave his words that he will not disclose his presence at his house. Griffin slept peacefully that night.

The next morning, Griffin awoke and as he was sure that Dr Kemp wouldn't disclose the facts he confided in him. Griffin told all his plans and secrets to Dr Kemp. Dr Kemp got to realise that Griffin wanted to establish a reign of terror and thus he wrote a note to Colonel Adye. Next happening was the arrival of Police to Kemp's house. Dr Kemp had betrayed Griffin and anyhow escape was made by Griffin.

He was in a furious rage as Kemp had cheated him. He went to the town and as he was in an awkward situation he was not in his senses. He was doubtful of his actions up next. Meanwhile Mr Wicksteed came into his way. Yet, there were no bad intentions with Wicksteed but in the fury of the betrayal Griffin hit him hard with an iron rod.

Mr Wicksteed was beaten to death by Griffin. No situation was there that could be justifiable for the incident so it could be said that Mr Wicksteed was a victim of the situations.

Q 2. The chapter also tries to explain that how Dr Kemp's treachery had hurt Griffin. Elaborate.

इस पाठ में डॉ केंप की ग्रिफिन को दी गई धोखेबाजी से आहत होने का भी वर्णन है। विस्तारपूर्वक बताएँ।

ग्रिफिन का डॉ केंप के घर में घुस जाना – डॉ केंप द्वारा उसे भोजन, कपड़ो और आश्रय प्रदान करना – ग्रिफिन का डॉ केंप पर बहुत भरोसा करना – अपने सारे राज बताना – डॉ केंप द्वारा कर्नल एडी को नोट लिखना – उन्हें ग्रिफिन को गिरफ्तार करने के लिए बुलाना – ग्रिफिन को पता चलना – डॉ केंप के द्वारा उसे धोखा देना – ग्रिफिन का वहाँ से भाग जाना – बरडॉक की सड़कों पर ग्रिफिन का आहत होना – उसका विश्वास टूटना – डॉ केंप के धोखा देने की वजह से ग्रिफिन की यह दशा होना।

Ans. When Griffin entered Dr Kemp's house, he demanded for food, clothes and shelter. All these were provided to him by Dr Kemp. Eventually, Griffin believed on

Dr Kemp and let him know all the secrets and all of his plans to Dr Kemp. Dr Kemp asked for every minute details from Griffin. While Griffin was taking rest during the night, Dr Kemp wrote a note to Colonel Adye regarding the ill-will of Griffin.

The next morning, Colonel Adye was there with full-fledged force. Griffin soon realised that Dr Kemp had cheated him and he made his escape from his house and came to the roads of Burdock, naked in chilly winter. He was disturbed by the idea that Dr Kemp, whom he trusted and told his secrets, had betrayed him.

He could not decide his next move and was in an utter shock at all the situation. His heart was weeping and he was shocked about all the happenings that were to take place. It all was due to Dr Kemp's cheat.

Q 3. Was Griffin sorry after what he had done? Has the narrator tried to present to us Griffin's side of story?

क्या कृत्य करने के बाद ग्रिफिन को अफसोस हुआ था? क्या कथाकार ने ग्रिफिन के पक्ष को भी कहानी में वर्णित करने की कोशिश की है?

डॉ कैंप का कर्नल एडी को बुलाना – पुलिस का बरडॉक की सड़कों पर से जाना – डॉ कैंप द्वारा धोखा देने के बाद ग्रिफिन का गुस्से से लाल होना – उसका सड़क पर आना और उसका एक बच्चे को उठाकर फेंक देना – उसे समझ नहीं आ रहा था कि वह क्या करे और क्या न करे – मि विकस्टीड को लोहे की रॉड से मारना – बाद में इस घटना पर ग्रिफिन का खुद अफसोस करना – कथाकार द्वारा ग्रिफिन के पक्ष की कहानी का भी वर्णन किया जाना।

Ans. When Dr Kemp called for Colonel Adye to catch Griffin then the latter got the idea of the betrayal. He managed to get away with the police and came out on the roads of Burdock. He was in an utmost fury about the situation and in that rage his mind had almost stopped working what to do and what not to. Griffin was seeming to be murderous in his rage. He threw out a child on the road breaking his ankle.

He moved forward and slowly. He was getting aware of the fact that a trap had been laid throughout. The town to get hold of him and he wouldn't be able to do what he wished. In the extreme rage, he saw Mr Wicksteed down the road and without any thinking he targetted him.

There was no evil intention in the mind of Mr Wicksteed yet he woas hit severely with an iron-rod. Even he was unaware of the reason of this blow, but it could be said that Griffin's rage did all this. Griffin had later remorsed over his blood spattered victim and he was shocked on his side. So, narrator had tried to present Griffin's story in this chapter intentionally.

The Siege of Kemp's House

The Threat Letter Arrives

The next day, Dr Kemp receives a letter written by Griffin. He threatens to murder Dr Kemp for his treachery. He warns others not to come in his way. Dr Kemp is scared but keeps himself cool. After that, he writes a note and asks his maid to take that to Colonel Adye.

The Servant Gets Ambushed

Colonel Adye came to his house. He informed Dr Kemp that his maid had been assaulted by the Invisible Man and the note taken away. Dr Kemp regretted his foolishness of sending the note. Suddenly, the windows of the house start getting smashed. The siege of Dr Kemp's house had begun.

Colonel Adye Gets Killed

Colonel Adye understands that they are no match for the Invisible Man. But Griffin was on the prowl. Colonel Adye asks for a revolver and after some hesitation, Dr Kemp gives up his own. Griffin wanted Colonel Adye to return to the house and had no intention of hurting him. But Colonel Adye tried to deceive Griffin and in the struggle, he was shot and died.

Help Arrives for Dr Kemp

Griffin had found an axe and started slamming the kitchen door. Dr Kemp knew that it will not hold Griffin much longer. The maid had arrived with two policemen. Dr Kemp informed them that Griffin had killed Colonel Adye and had a revolver. They got pokers and waited for Griffin.

The Siege of Kemp's House

धमकी भरा पत्र मिलना

अगले दिन Dr Kemp (डॉ कैंप) को Griffin (ग्रिफिन) का लिखा हुआ पत्र मिला। पत्र में उसने डॉ कैंप को जान से मारने की धमकी दी थी। उसने दूसरे लोगों को उसके रास्ते में ना आने की चेतावनी दी थी। डॉ कैंप डर गए थे, परंतु उन्होंने अपने आप को संभाला। उसके बाद उन्होंने Colonel Adye (कर्नल एडी) को एक पत्र लिखा और अपनी नौकरानी को उसे देने के लिए भेजा।

नौकर का पकड़ लिया जाना

कर्नल एडी उनके घर आए। उन्होंने डॉ कैंप को बताया कि अदृश्य आदमी द्वारा नौकरानी पर हमला हुआ है और उससे पत्र छीन लिया गया है। डॉ कैंप को पत्र भेजने की अपनी बेवकूफी पर खेद हुआ। अचानक घर की खिड़कियाँ टूटने लगीं। डॉ कैंप के घर में अवरोध शुरू हो चुका था।

कर्नल एडी की मृत्यु हो जाना

कर्नल एडी जानते थे कि अदृश्य आदमी से मुकाबला बिल्कुल आसान नहीं होगा। परंतु ग्रिफिन शिकार की खोज में घूम रहा था। कर्नल एडी ने बंदूक माँगी और डॉ. कैंप ने थोड़ी हिचकिचाहट के बाद कर्नल एडी को अपनी बंदूक दे दी। ग्रिफिन चाहता था कि कर्नल एडी घर वापस चले जाएँ और उन्हें नुकसान पहुँचाने की उसकी कोई इच्छा नहीं थी। परंतु कर्नल एडी ने ग्रिफिन के साथ चालाकी करने की कोशिश की और संघर्ष के दौरान उन्हें गोली लग गई और वह मर गए।

डॉ कैंप के लिए सहायता का प्रबंध हो जाना

ग्रिफिन ने Axe (कुल्हाड़ी) खोज ली थी तथा रसोईघर के दरवाजे को पीटना शुरू कर दिया था। डॉ कैंप जानते थे कि ग्रिफिन किसी भी वक्त उन तक पहुँच सकता था। नौकरानी ने दो पुलिसवालों को बुला लिया था। डॉ कैंप ने उन्हें बताया कि ग्रिफिन ने कर्नल एडी को मार दिया है और उसके पास बंदूक भी है। उन्होंने अपने हाथ में डंडे ले लिए और ग्रिफिन की प्रतीक्षा करने लगे।

Griffin Gets Hurt and Escapes

Griffin gets in brandishing the revolver and the axe. Though ill-equipped, the policemen started to struggle. A shot was fired, but missed its spot. The other policeman brought the poker down and the revolver fell from Griffin's hand. He said that he didn't want to hurt the two. But they replied that they wanted to catch him. Then Griffin hurt one of them with the axe. However, the other one was quick to react and hit the air hard. The poker hit Griffin's hand and broke it. Griffin escaped. Dr Kemp and the maid also escaped.

ग्रिफिन को चोट लगना और भाग निकलना

ग्रिफिन बंदूक व कुल्हाड़ी लहराता हुआ आगे बढ़ा। कम सामग्री होने के बाद भी, पुलिसवालों ने संघर्ष शुरू किया। एक गोली चली, परंतु निशाने से चूक गई। एक अन्य पुलिसवाला डंडे को नीचे लाया और ग्रिफिन के हाथ से बंदूक गिर गई। उसने कहा कि वह उन दोनों को नुकसान नहीं पहुँचाना चाहता। परंतु उन्होंने उत्तर दिया कि वे उसे पकड़ना चाहते हैं। फिर ग्रिफिन ने उनमें से एक को कुल्हाड़ी से मारा। हालाँकि, दूसरे ने तीव्रता से प्रतिक्रिया की और हवा में जोर से वार किया। डंडा ग्रिफिन के हाथ में लगा और वह टूट गया। ग्रिफिन वहाँ से भाग गया। डॉ कैंप व नौकरानी भी वहाँ से भाग गए।

Word Meaning

Missive – पत्र
Execution – फाँसी देना/मारना
Hoax – अफवाह
Explicit – सुस्पष्ट
Assaulted – हमला करना
Contemplating – सोच-विचार करना
Whack – जोर से प्रहार करना
Hard by – पास में होना
Sprawling – चारों ओर फैलते हुए
Wrested – झटके में लेना
Sullenly – नाखुश होकर
Scruting – छानबीन करना
Tumultous – उपद्रवी
Splintering – चीरना
Fender – चोट से बचने का साधन
Rattling – तीव्र गति से
Epoch – लंबा वक्त
Armour – कवच
Prosaic – साधारण
Vengeance – बदला
Hysterics – भयंकर डर होना
Wreckage – नाश होना
Confound – पराजित करना
Desisted – रोक लेना
Clumsily – भद्दे तरीके से
Multitudinous– कई हिस्सों से बना होना
Parleying – बातचीत करना
Writhed – मुड़ा हुआ
Pursuant – से जुड़ा हुआ
Shuddered – रोंगटे खड़े कर देना
Penultimate – अंत से पहले
Staggered – लड़खड़ाते हुए

Important Questions

Questions based on the Plot of the Chapter

Q 1. Dr Kemp acted foolishly when he thought that he would act as bait and lure Griffin out. Comment.

डॉ केंप ने मूर्खतापूर्ण व्यवहार किया जब उन्होंने सोचा कि वह एक चारे के रूप में कार्य करेंगे और ग्रिफिन को अपनी तरफ आकर्षित करके उसे पकड़ लेंगे। टिप्पणी करें।

केंप के धोखा देने के बाद ग्रिफिन का इरादा खतरनाक हो जाना – उसकी मंशा बदला लेना – केंप को एक धमकी भरा पत्र लिखना – उन्हें जान से मारने की धमकी देना – पत्र पाकर केंप द्वारा एडी को एक नोट लिखना – ग्रिफिन को पकड़ने का सबसे सुनहरा मौका – पत्र एडी से पहले ग्रिफिन के हाथ लगना और उसको योजना की भनक लगना – एडी का केंप को कहना कि यह एक बेकार योजना थी।

Ans. Baffled by Kemp's treachery, Griffin was so filled by rage that was close to furious. He was damn threatening to him. He wandered on the roads of town and happened to see the trap that was laid for him. He became so murderous that had no limit. He thought of a plan. He wrote a missive addressed to Kemp. In that missive, he threatened Kemp that he would have to meet his death for the act that he had done with Griffin.

He also wrote that if someone would try to come in between, he would be punished with death too. When Kemp received the missive and went through it, terror had shrieked him from within. He took a deep breathe and decided to stay calm.

He wrote another letter to Colonel Adye and sent it through his maid. In that letter, he had mentioned that that's the best chance to catch Griffin. He would come to see Kemp for sure and he must be trapped then at Kemp's house. The letter was snatched by Griffin from the maid and all the plan was out before him crystal clear.

When Adye told it to Kemp, he realised that the writing was a foolish act and he should have done it never. Now, the plan was out Griffin will be severely furious.

Q 2. Colonel Adye tried to play a hero and unfortunately lost his life. Elaborate.

कर्नल एडी ने नायक बनने की कोशिश की और दुर्भाग्यवश अपनी जान गँवा दी। वर्णन करें।

ग्रिफिन का पत्र कैंप को मिलना – जान से मारने की धमकी होना – एडी का कैंप को मदद का आश्वासन देना – एडी का अपनी सुरक्षा के लिए कैंप की बंदूक के साथ बाहर जाना – ग्रिफिन द्वारा एडी की बंदूक छीनकर उन्हें कैंप के घर लाना – एडी का कैंप को बचाने की कोशिश करना – गुस्से में ग्रिफिन द्वारा एडी को गोली मार देना – एडी की नायक बनने की वह कोशिश उनकी जान ले गई थी।

Ans. On receiving the letter packed with threat of death to Kemp, he was baffled. He started to look out for ways. He wrote a note to Colonel Adye in which he elaborated his plans. Unfortunately, that letter couldn't reach the destination and fell in the hands of the Invisible Man.

He read it out and changed the plan. Somehow, Adye reached Kemp's house and saw the letter of Griffin. Kemp was threatened to death.

Adye told him not to get worried as he would help him. In order to provide him security, Adye had to go out and had to call some more policemen who could be able to help Kemp. Adye asked for the gun from Kemp as his own security measures. After hesitation, Kemp gave him his gun. Adye went out and stopped by Griffin.

Griffin also took over his gun and pointed it to him. Adye was then asked to go back to Kemp's house as Griffin wanted to kill Kemp. Both reached the house and Adye tried to become a hero as he had promised security to Kemp.

Griffin did not like the idea of negotiation by Adye and eventually, he was shot dead and lost his life. So, being hero costed Adye to his life.

Q 3. What does the letter from Griffin reveal about his nature?

ग्रिफिन के पत्र से उसके स्वभाव के बारे में क्या पता चलता है?

ग्रिफिन द्वारा कैंप को धमकी भरा पत्र लिखना – उनको जान से मारने की धमकी देना – ग्रिफिन को धोखा देने वाले लोगों से नफरत होना – ग्रिफिन का कानून को न मानना और इसलिए ऐसा करना उसके लिए नई बात न होना – कैंप को सबसे बुरे हालात में पहुँचाना तय कर लेना – ग्रिफिन के गुस्से का भी अंत न होना – धोखेबाजों को मौत की सजा देने का फैसला।

Ans. Griffin wrote a letter to Dr Kemp. The letter was written for the latter had treachered the former whom he promised the non-disclosing of his hiding in his house. The letter revealed the rage of Griffin. The cheating of Kemp had disturbed him deeply and he was not in the position to assert his steps.

He went back to his determined course of actions that was establishing a reign of terror. He decided to murder Dr Kemp to start with. He also wrote if someone ever tried to come his way, he too would be slayed.

This was the start of the terror and he had signalled the arrival of the fury. As we know Griffin was a lawless person, so whatever he had written in letter was surely on the cards. He would never be in suppressing mood of his actions. He would do the worst-possible to Kemp.

He was so baffled by the cheater that he would not be stopping himself before taking the life of Kemp. This letter was significant for its cause that Griffin hated those who had ever cheated him. He was always in a mood to punish the cheaters with death and so was the case with Kemp.

The Hunter Hunted

Mr Heelas doesn't Allow Dr Kemp Shelter

Mr Heelas was a non-believer in the Invisible Man's story. He was awakened by the sound of smashing windows. He looked across at Dr Kemp's house and found it to be fully deserted. Dr Kemp asked for shelter from Mr Heelas which he outrightly denied for the fear of the Invisible Man.

Dr Kemp Runs for his Life

Dr Kemp ran for his life for he knew that Griffin was after him and wanted to murder him. Suddenly, he saw a couple of workmen on the road. He shoutedly told them about the Invisible Man.

Griffin Reaps What He had Sown

As others were trying to defend Dr Kemp, Griffin started beating him. Suddenly, a labourer hits him with a spade. Griffin starts to bleed. They all held him down and he started crying for mercy.

Dr Kemp asked everybody to leave him. However, it was too late and Griffin had died in the struggle. After his death, his body became visible again. But the gifted physicist met a tragic end.

The Hunter Hunted

मि हीलास का डॉ केंप को आश्रय नहीं देना

Mr Heelas (मि हीलास) अदृश्य आदमी की कहानी में यकीन नहीं करते थे। वह खिड़कियों के टूटने की आवाज सुनकर जाग गए थे। उन्होंने Dr Kemp (डॉ केंप) के घर की ओर देखा और उसे पूरी तरह उजड़ा पाया। डॉ केंप ने मि हीलास से Shelter (आश्रय) माँगा, जो उन्होंने अदृश्य आदमी के डर से बिल्कुल मना कर दिया।

डॉ केंप का अपनी जान बचाने के लिए भागना

डॉ केंप अपनी जान बचाने के लिए भागने लगे क्योंकि वह जानते थे कि ग्रिफिन उनके पीछे था और उन्हें मारना चाहता था। अचानक उन्होंने सड़क पर कुछ Laborers (मजदूरों) को देखा। उन्होंने चिल्लाकर उन्हें अदृश्य आदमी के बारे में बताया।

ग्रिफिन द्वारा अपने किए का फल भोगना

अन्य लोग डॉ केंप को बचाने की कोशिश कर रहे थे, और इसी बीच, ग्रिफिन ने उन्हें पीटना शुरू कर दिया। अचानक एक मजदूर ने उस पर अपने Spade (फावड़े) से वार किया। ग्रिफिन के शरीर से खून बहने लगा। सब लोगों ने ग्रिफिन को पकड़ लिया और उसने दया के लिए रोना शुरू कर दिया था।

डॉ केंप ने सब लोगों को उसे छोड़ देने के लिए कहा। लेकिन बहुत देर हो चुकी थी और इस संघर्ष में ग्रिफिन की मृत्यु हो गई थी। मृत्यु के पश्चात् उसका शरीर फिर से दिखने लगा था। लेकिन एक प्रतिभावान वैज्ञानिक की दुखद मृत्यु हो चुकी थी।

Word Meaning

Evades	– भाग जाना	Laburnum	– एक प्रकार का पौधा
Abutted	– नजदीक होना	Pelting	– तेजी से भागना
Precipitately	– तेजी से	Intervened	– हस्तक्षेप करना
Dazzling	– चकित कर देने वाला	Gaunt	– भयानक
Spurt	– तेजी से निकलना	Fag	– कड़ी मेहनत करना
Alley	– सकरी गली	Appartition	– अचानक सामने आना
Tumultous	– उथल-पुथल मचना	Vociferation	– कड़ा विरोध करना
Savage	– निर्दयी होना	Stalwart	– मांसल होना
Shamming	– नकल करना	Bruised	– आघात लगना
Hazy	– धुंधला होना	Intricate	– उलझा हुआ
Battered	– बुरी स्थिति में होना	Garnets	– लाल पत्थर
Tawdry	– बेस्वाद होना		

Important Questions

Questions based on the Plot of the Chapter

Q 1. Why did Mr Heelas not provide shelter to Dr Kemp in his time of need?

मि हीलास ने डॉ केंप को जरूरत के समय अपने घर में आश्रय क्यों नहीं लेने दिया?

ग्रिफिन का डॉ केंप के घर जाना – कर्नल एडी का उसको निशाने पर लेना – मि हीलास का डॉ केंप का पड़ोसी होना – हीलास का अदृश्य आदमी पर विश्वास नहीं करना – अपने घर में आराम से सोना – डॉ केंप के घर पर ग्रिफिन का हमला करना – उनके घर को तबाह कर देना – ग्रिफिन का अपने घर से भाग जाना – मदद के लिए मि हीलास के घर छिप जाना – मि हीलास का ग्रिफिन की वजह से डॉ केंप को अपने घर में न रुकने देने का निर्णय करना।

Ans. The letter, filled with threat reached Dr Kemp and after some time, Griffin himself reached Kemp's house with Colonel Adye on his gun point. As the letter was all about the death of Dr Kemp so Griffin was making the course of action accordingly. Mr Heelas was the neighbour of Dr Kemp and he was never having the belief that there could be the existence of an Invisible Man in the world. He was peaceful in his house irrespective of the whole folk of Burdock.

During his sleep, there was a smash on the window panes of Dr Kemp's house and the moment it stopped the sleep of Mr Heelas broke off.

As he was awakened, he saw that the house of Dr Kemp was almost in ruins. He asked for the reason and as he got to know that all these were due to Invisible Man, he started believing him. He also got to know that he was behind Dr Kemp.

That very moment, Mr Heelas saw that Dr Kemp was heading towards his house in the need of shelter. Mr Heelas didn't allow him to come inside as he was afraid of the fury that Invisible Man could produce to him. That's why Mr Heelas refused Dr Kemp for help.

Q 2. Describe the scene when Dr Kemp was running away to save his life.

उस स्थिति का वर्णन करें, जब डॉ केंप अपनी जान बचाने के लिए भाग रहे थे।

ग्रिफिन का डॉ केंप के पीछे भागना – डॉ केंप का अपनी जान बचाने हेतु भागना – पहाड़ी के रास्ते पर जाना – ग्रिफिन को मुश्किल होना – उसके पीछा करने में बाजार से होते हुए जाना – प्रत्येक घर पर दस्तक देना – उन्हें मदद मिल सके – वहाँ से फिर कार्यस्थल पर जाना – फिर निश्चय करना – पुलिस स्टेशन जाना – बाद में इरादा बदल लिया जाना।

Ans. He was threatened to life by Griffin. The threat comes to be true when Dr Kemp was chased by Griffin. Now, all that Griffin had to do was to go and wander for his life in the outer territory. He was running to save his life from the lurking death and he made all the possible efforts for that.

He started to run on the hilly areas where there was a difficult walk all the way. He did it so deliberately that Griffin felt a difficulty in moving. None opened the door for him and he was running like a mad man.

He crossed the working sites where a number of labourers were busy with their work, but Griffin was chasing him hard. Dr Kemp thought to go to police station but changed the idea later on for good.

The Epilogue

Mr Marvel Makes a Fortune

The narration shifts again after the tragic death of the Invisible Man and takes us to an inn owned by a short, fat guy. It is none other than Mr Marvel himself. He named the inn "The Invisible Man". The authorities were unable to prove whose money Mr Marvel had. So, he got to keep all of it. Mr Marvel also made a fortune by telling his side of the story.

Mr Marvel Still has the Three Books

If one asks Mr Marvel about the three books, he admits that they existed but he hasn't got them. He blames Dr Kemp for spreading this rumour. However, the three books are with Mr Marvel only. He had hid them in a marsh and now they lie in his cupboard. He takes a hard look at them daily in the hope of understanding the coded language. But alas! He is unable to do so. Looking at the books, he wonders what secrets are written in them and what will happen one day if he also becomes invisible.

Word Meaning

Corpulent	– मोटा	Sporadic	– अनियमित
Visage	– व्यक्ति का चेहरा	Trove	– कीमती चीजों का संग्रह
Asseverations	– गंभीरतापूर्वक	Reminiscences	– यादें
Pensive	– ख्यालों में खोए रहना	Furtively	– गुप्त रूप से
Eminent	– प्रसिद्ध	Decorum	– अनुशासन
Parismony	– कंजूस होना	Gin	– मदिरा
Tinged	– कम मात्रा में मिलाना	Solemnly	– शांति से
Sojourned	– क्षणिक विश्रामालय	Glroating	– खुश होना
Knit	– ठीक तरीके से लगा हुआ	Fished unceasingly	– लगातार खोजना

The Epilogue

मि मार्वेल की किस्मत खुल जाना

वर्णनकर्ता अदृश्य आदमी की मौत के बाद हमारा ध्यान पलट देता है तथा एक मोटे व नाटे कद के व्यक्ति के धर्मशाला की ओर ले जाता है। यह व्यक्ति कोई और नहीं बल्कि खुद मि मार्वेल हैं। इस धर्मशाला का नाम उन्होंने The Invisible Man ('द इनविजिबल मैन') रखा है। धर्मशाला के बनने में लगने वाली सारी रकम मार्वेल को कहाँ से मिली है यह कोई भी पता नहीं कर पाया था। व इसी वजह से सारा पैसा मार्वेल को ही दे दिया गया। मि मार्वेल दूसरे लोगों को भी अपनी कहानी सुनाया करता था।

मि मार्वेल के पास अभी भी वह तीन किताबें होना

अगर कोई Mr Marvel (मि मार्वेल) से पूछता कि क्या उसके पास वो तीन किताबें हैं तो वह मना कर देता था। वह इस अफवाह के लिए डॉ कैंप को दोषी मानता था। वस्तुत: वह तीनों किताबें मि मार्वेल के ही पास थी। उसने उन्हें कहीं छिपा दिया था और अब वे किताबें उसके घर की आलमारी में थी। वह रोज उन किताबों पर एक नजर डालता ताकि वह उसमें लिखी चीजें समझ सके। लेकिन उसे अफसोस के अलावा और कुछ भी हाथ नहीं लगा था। उन किताबों में जो राज की बातें लिखी थी उसे समझने में वह दिलचस्पी लेता और सोचता था कि अगर वह भी एक दिन अदृश्य हो जाए तो क्या होगा।

Important Questions

Questions based on the Plot of the Chapter

Q 1. Why do you think Mr Marvel had named his inn "The Invisible Man"?

मि मार्वेल ने धर्मशाला का नाम 'द इनविजिबल मैन' क्यों रखा था?

मि मार्वेल पर ग्रिफिन द्वारा भरोसा करना – उसे धन व किताबें देना – मि मार्वेल का ग्रिफिन से बचने के लिए भाग जाना और जेल में जाकर छिप जाना – इस बीच ग्रिफिन की मृत्यु होना – सारा धन व किताबें मि मार्वेल के पास रह जाना – मि मार्वेल का उस पैसे से धर्मशाला खोलना – धर्मशाला का नाम 'द इनविजिबल मैन' रखना।

Ans. Mr Marvel was a carefree man and he loved to enjoy nature at its best. He was sitting near a ditch casually when Griffin met him for the first time. When Griffin met him he was so taken back by him that he decided to make him his friend. Griffin confide in him and it was obvious that he was to be used as a sidekick. Mr Marvel wanted to leave him, but as there was the threat of life to him, he couldn't leave him. He was having money and the three books of Griffin with him when he left Griffin for good.

He was chased by the Invisible Man, but fortunately he locked himself inside a cell in the prison on his own request to the policeman. He hid himself and all the while Griffin was searching for him to kill him and to cover his three books.

As there were adverse things that happened with Griffin and eventually he died. Then the three books were with Mr Marvel and the money that Griffin had left with him were also his. When the authorities try to enquire about the source of money, there couldn't be revealed anything. So, all the money was left behind with Mr Marvel and he opened an inn with this money. So, Mr Marvel named the inn "The Invisible man".

Q 2. Do you think that Mr Marvel can make use of Griffin's work? Justify your answer.

क्या आपको लगता है कि मि मार्वेल ग्रिफिन के अविष्कार का इस्तेमाल कर सकता है? अपने उत्तर का उचित वर्णन किजिए।

मि मार्वेल के पास ग्रिफिन का सारा धन और उसकी तीन किताबें होना – उन किताबों में ग्रिफिन के प्रयोग की सारी जानकारी कूट भाषा में लिखी होना – मि मार्वेल की कोशिश कि वह कूट व सांकेतिक भाषा को समझ पाए – मि मार्वेल के अशिक्षित होने की वजह से ऐसा असंभव होना – ग्रिफिन के आविष्कार का किसी भी तरह से इस्तेमाल न कर पाना।

Ans. After the death of Griffin, Mr Marvel had all of his money and the three valuable books of him. These books were very much important for Griffin. The chase that Griffin had given to Mr Marvel was not only for his life but for his three valuable books also. These three books were related to the ways and keys of the experiment that Griffin had performed for his invisibility and that's why it was needed for him the most.

These books were written in a certain code that only the Invisible Man could understand and as Mr Marvel had these books, there was no possibility of the deciphering of the code that lies in that books.

It was because of the fact that the man was not a literate one and his skills were limited to the table of dinner only. Whenever Mr Marvel found time he would try to go through the books and his intention was to decipher the underlying code, but alas it was never possible with a man like him who didn't know the abc of the writings. So, we could say that there is no possibility that Mr Marvel could ever make use of Griffin's discovery.

Questions based on the Character Sketch

Q 1. In the epilogue of the novel, we see Mr Marvel as an opportunist and as a selfish man. What impression does he leave on you?

इस पाठ मि मार्वेल को एक स्वार्थी और अवसरवादी व्यक्ति के रूप में प्रस्तुत किया गया है। आप उसके बारे में क्या राय रखते हो?

मि मार्वेल को ग्रिफिन द्वारा भरोसेमंद दोस्त बनाना – मि मार्वेल का हमेशा भागने की कोशिश करना – एक बार ग्रिफिन का धन व किताबें लेकर भाग जाना – ग्रिफिन के धन से धर्मशाला बनाना – किताबों का राज अपने तक सीमित रखना – इससे साबित होना कि ग्रिफिन स्वार्थी और अवसरवादी था।

Ans. From the beginning of Mr Marvel's episode, in the whole scenario, he had played various characters altogether. In the beginning, he had been a careless and casual person who would like to sit anywhere and would be busy with his own musings. When Griffin had met him for the first time, he was sitting near a ditch and was busy with the selection of the pair of shoes that he should wear. When Griffin made him his sidekick, he was always looking to flee away from him.

It was his threat that kept him very bound to Griffin otherwise he would have made his escape when he found an opportunity. That really reflected the idea that he had been an opportune totally when all the money remained with him. He made the full use of it and opened an inn.

He kept all the books with him too that showed that he was so selfish. Had he parted with the book only to Dr Kemp then it might be of a great use to the society, but his self didn't allow him to do so. It was the proof of his selfishness.

QUESTION DIGEST

Questions based on the Plot/Theme/Event

Q 1. The stranger's arrival at the inn was an unusual event. Moreover, his behaviour was very rude. Why did Mrs Hall put up with the antics of the stranger then?

अजनबी का धर्मशाला आना एक असामान्य घटना थी। इसके अतिरिक्त उसका व्यवहार सख्त था। इतने विरोधाभासों के बाद भी मिसेज हॉल अजनबी को क्यों सहन कर रही थी?

Ans. It was February when the stranger arrived at the "Coach and Horses" inn in Iping. It was a time of biting cold with wind and snow. Not many people visited Iping in winters and hence, the inn business must have been low. To have a guest at that time of the year was something unheard of.

Mrs Hall was very happy. Also, the stranger did no bargaining. He gave her two gold coins. However, he was a very rude character. He snubbed her many times and even destroyed some property of the inn. But Mrs Hall kept her cool because every time she confronted him for the damage, he told her to bill him down. The money kept coming in and Mrs Hall didn't want to lose the customer until it was holiday season again.

Q 2. Describe the appearance of the stranger when he arrived at the inn. Why was Mrs Hall scared out of her wits by his appearance?

धर्मशाला में आने पर अजनबी की वेशभूषा का वर्णन कीजिए। मिसेज हॉल उसकी वेशभूषा को देखकर क्यों घबरा गई थी?

Ans. The stranger was wrapped from head to toe and the large hat that he wore hid every inch of his face but the shiny tip of his nose. Mrs Hall gave him a room. When she went there, she noticed that his clothes were still on. He was also wearing big blue spectacles with sidelights and had a bush side-whisker over his coat-collar that completely hid his cheeks and face.

The next time, she went into the room, she saw that the stranger had taken off his overcoat and hat. He was holding a handkerchief to his mouth that hid the lower portion of his jaw and that made his voice muffled. But what was more startling was that his whole face, except his pink nose, was covered in bandages. His hair went through the bandages and gave him the most grotesque appearance. It gave Mrs Hall the shock of her life.

Q 3. Describe Teddy Henfrey's first impression of the Invisible Man.

टेडी हेनफ्रे के अदृश्य आदमी से जुड़े प्रथम अनुभव क्या थे?

Ans. The Invisible Man was sleeping when Mrs Hall came with Mr Teddy Henfrey, the clock-jobber. He woke up with a startle. When Teddy entered, he was 'taken aback' by the bandaged appearance of the man.

Getting his consent, Mr Teddy Henfrey proceeded to work. But he worked as slow as possible. He wanted to know more about the stranger. The stranger kept staring at him and the silence of the room made Teddy nervous. He tried to start a conversation, but the stranger snubbed him and said that he was wasting time and he should concentrate on his work and leave. Mr Teddy was really annoyed at this behaviour.

He was the first one to spread rumors about the Invisible Man. He thought that the man was bandaged as he was trying to run away from the police. He told Mr Hall the same thing and asked him to take a note of the situation.

Q 4. "It's a rummy case altogether." What was the 'rummy case'? What possible explanation was given for it?

"यह अपने आप में ताश के पत्तों का समूह है।" इस कथन में "ताश के पत्ते जैसा" कौन है? इसके लिए संभावित कारण क्या थे?

Ans. The unusual stranger was staying in the 'Coach and Horses' inn at Iping and eagerly waiting for his luggage to arrive. Fearenside, the cart-driver, brought the luggage and was standing outside the inn with Mr Hall. The Invisible Man came running down. Just as he was about to reach the cart, Fearenside's dog attacked him. His glove and trousers were torn apart. But he said that he was not hurt.

Later, Mr Teddy and Fearenside met at the bar and discussed the incident. Fearenside said that the man was black as when he saw through the tore trousers, he expected that his skin would be pinkish. But it was complete blackness. Mr Teddy Henfrey said that it was a 'rummy case' because his nose was pink.

Fearenside said that the man was probably a piebald. He thought that the man was half-breed which led to spots.

Q 5. "It's a most remarkable story." What made Mr Bunting say this?

"यह एक अद्‌भुत कहानी है।" मि बंटिंग ने ऐसा क्यों कहा?

Ans. Mr Cuss, the general practitioner at Iping village, was a curious cat by nature. He heard about the stranger staying at Iping. The news of him being covered in bandages excited his professional interest. He was also jealous to learn that the stranger had numerous bottles of chemicals with him.

He made the excuse of a subscription and was able to arrange a meeting with him. Unfortunately, the interview ended abruptly and he ran straight to another bar where Mr Bunting was sitting. He told Mr Bunting that the stranger got irritated with him and what happened next made him shiver and run thinking that he had gone insane. Actually, Griffin had scared him by his show of empty sleeve and poking his nose with his invisible hand. Though Mr Bunting looked suspiciously at Mr Cuss, he said that it was a most remarkable story.

Q 6. How did Griffin move about in the village of Iping? What were the rumors revolving around regarding his bandages?

ग्रिफिन आइपिंग गाँव में कैसे चलता था? गाँव में उसके पट्टियाँ बाँधने की क्या अफवाह उड़ रही थी?

Ans. Griffin's behaviour was very unusual. He did not go to church. Somedays, he would be continuously busy with his work and on others, he would just pace in his room. His temper was very unpredictable. Moreover, he rarely went abroad by daylight and had no communication with the outside world. However, he always kept himself covered whether it was cold or hot. He would walk on the loneliest paths and among the shades of the trees. People often got scared when they met him walking down the street and his appearance made him the talk of the town. Mrs Hall kept telling everybody that he was an 'experimental investigator'. But many also believed that he was a criminal trying to hide himself in bandages. Some thought that he was an anarchist. Then there were people like Fearenside who believed that he was a piebald.

Q 7. Describe the burglary that took place at Mr Bunting's house in your own words.

मि बंटिंग के घर हुई चोरी का वर्णन अपने शब्दों में करो।

Ans. In the wake hours of Whit Monday, Mrs Bunting was woken up by a strong impression that the door of the bedroom had opened and closed. When she was assured that there was an intruder in the house, she woke Mr Bunting up.

Mr Bunting didn't act hastingly and after making sure that a burglar was at work, armed himself with a poker and went down. The couple could hear the study drawers being opened and rustle of papers. A match was lit in the study. Mr Bunting tried to peep but could spot no one. Suddenly, they heard the chink of money and realised that the burglar had found the reserve.

Mr Bunting barged into the room only to see that the room was perfectly empty. They were completely astonished. The candle was lit, the money was gone, but there was no one in the room. Then they ran towards the sound coming from the kitchen but not a soul was to be found.

Q 8. "My good old furniture! 'Twas in that very chair my poor dear mother used to sit when I was a little girl. To think it should rise up against me now!" What had happened to Mrs Hall's furniture?

"मेरा बढ़िया व प्यारा फर्नीचर। इसी कुर्सी पर मेरी माँ बैठा करती थी जब मैं छोटी थी। मुझे समझ नहीं आ रहा कि यह मुझे मारने के लिए उठेगी।" मिसेज हॉल के फर्नीचर को क्या हुआ था?

Ans. In the early hours of Whit Monday, the Halls woke up to attend a private matter. They were to add sarsaparilla to their beer. Mr Hall went upstairs to get the bottle and was surprised to notice that the stranger's door was open. Then he found the front door open which they had bolted last night.

Curiously, he knocked at the door of the room but the room was empty. He called Mrs Hall up. All the stranger's clothes were lying here and there. Mrs Hall touched them and concluded from the coldness that he had been out for long.

Just then, the bed clothes gathered themselves and jumped aside. The stranger's hat attacked Mrs Hall's face. The chair came to life and charged at Mrs Hall. The chair threw the couple outside. Mrs Hall thought that her furniture was haunted and it was the stranger who had put spirits in them.

Q 9. Who was Mr Sandy Wadgers? What impression does he leave on the reader?

मि सैंडी वैजर्स कौन था? पाठकों पर वह क्या प्रभाव छोड़ते हैं?

Ans. Mr Sandy Wadgers was a blacksmith in the village of Iping. He was the first one to be called by the couple when they were attacked by the furniture in the stranger's room. He was a knowing man and very resourceful. He was superstitious and after hearing about the attack, concluded that it was black magic. He appears to be a man who is calm and thinks before taking decisions. He wanted to get his facts right before dusting in the room of the stranger.

He is also very firm and resolute. He told Mr Hall to demand an explanation from the stranger. Later we also learn of his bravery when we see him fighting with the Invisible Man. However, the shock of getting beaten by the Invisible Man is too much to bear for him and he kept himself locked up in his house.

Q 10. Why did the narrator say that Mrs Hall had the better of the Invisible Man in the bar?

कथाकार ने ऐसा क्यों कहा कि बार में मिसेज हॉल अजनबी पर भारी पड़ रही थी?

Ans. After the attack by the furniture, the Halls were thinking of throwing out the stranger. Mrs Hall was very upset at what had happened. Moreover, when Mr Hall demanded an explanation, the stranger was very rude and asked to be left alone.

The Halls had enough of his temper and Mrs Hall decided that she would not serve him any longer. She could hear the stranger in rage and ringing the bell, but she was resolute. When the stranger asked for her, she immediately demanded her payment and asked him to keep his swearing to himself. Her furiousness made the stranger back down and it was felt in the bar that Mrs Hall had the better of him. She also accused him of stealing and demanded explanation for his unusual disappearances.

Q 11. The people of Iping village were no match for the Invisible Man. What happened when they all tried to get him arrested?

आइपिंग गाँव के लोग अदृश्य आदमी को जोड़ नहीं दे सकते थे। जब सबने मिलकर अजनबी को पकड़ने की कोशिश की तो क्या हुआ था?

Ans. The stranger was very furious when Mrs Hall accused him of stealing money from Mr Bunting's house. In a fit of rage, the stranger unveiled himself. The inn was not prepared for this sight and the panicked people ran outside. Mr Jaffers came with the warrant to arrest him. He said that head or no head, he would arrest the man. A fight ensued between the stranger and him and Mr Jaffers got brutally beaten up. However, with the help of Mr Hall, Mr Wadgers and others, the Invisible Man was subdued. But before anyone could suspect, the Invisible Man was off his clothes and the people were fighting an invisible figure.

Obviously, they were no match for him. Anyone who tried to catch him was hit. Mr Jaffers tried his best to get a hold of him but was so forcefully hit that he was rendered flat on the gravel.

Q 12. "Pull yourself together," said the Voice, "for you have to do the job I've chosen for you." Why had the Invisible Man chosen Mr Marvel? Did Mr Marvel prove his worth?

आवाज ने कहा, ''अपने आप को सँभालो क्योंकि मैंने अपना काम करने के लिए तुम्हें चुना है।'' अजनबी ने मि मार्वेल को क्यों चुना? क्या मार्वेल अपनी उपयोगिता साबित कर पाए?

Ans. After running away from the Iping village, the Invisible Man was filled with murderous rage. He was hungry and without shelter or clothes in the bittering cold. It was then he spotted Mr Thomas Marvel. He perceived Mr Marvel to be an outcast like him and thought that he could be of great help. He wanted Mr Marvel to aid him and act as a sidekick. The Invisible Man promised him rewards for his services. But he also threatened him of dire consequences if Mr Marvel tried to cheat him.

However, Mr Marvel was an opportunist. He tried to run away from him at Iping but was caught. He also tried to reveal the secret to a mariner at Port Stowe. He managed to escape from Griffin at Burdock with his priceless three books and all his heist. Thus, he was a poor sidekick and very much responsible for Griffin's downfall.

Q 13. Mr Huxter had a very sharp eye and was a person quick to react. Describe how he tried to intercept Mr Marvel but failed. What impression does he leave on the reader?

मि हक्सटर की आँखें तेज थी और वे बहुत चौकन्ने थे। उन्होंने मार्वेल को किस तरह से वर्णन करने की कोशिश की और असफल हुए? पाठकों पर वह क्या प्रभाव डालते हैं?

Ans. The day when Mr Marvel arrived at the inn, Mr Huxter was whitewashing. As he noticed a stranger with a shabby appearance near the inn, he got his eyes fixed. At once, he realised that the short man was up to something. He concluded that he was a thief and started chasing him. However, his chase was brought to an abrupt halt by Griffin.

Mr Huxter had a very keen eye which is clear from his perceptions about Mr Marvel. He was also quick to react and took decisions swiftly. At first, he encounters him telling people that if the dog had bitten the stranger, he must cauterise it. He is also reasonable and curious as he could not believe in the Invisible Man. He was also brave. He not only tried to stop Mr Marvel but also tried to catch Griffin.

Q 14. Mr Cuss and Mr Bunting tried to play investigators but Griffin humiliated them and still managed to escape with his three precious books. Elaborate.

मि कस व मि बंटिंग जाँचकर्ता बनने की कोशिश कर रहे थे। ग्रिफिन ने उनकी बेइज्जती भी की व अपनी तीन किताबों के साथ निकल गया। वर्णन करें।

Ans. The Invisible Man had escaped from the 'Coach and Horses' even though many villagers tried to stop him. They were all perplexed and nothing knew about his true identity. Mr Cuss and Mr Bunting appear to be the most lettered persons of the village. They started to investigate the Invisible Man's belongings. Mr Marvel was successful in providing Griffin entry into the room. Before they could realise, Griffin was banging their heads. He was angry and wanted his books. The two were no match for him and easily gave in. He made Mr Cuss wear a kilt and took away all the vicar's clothes.

Aided by Mr Marvel, Griffin was able to get away with his books. In this way, he humiliated and ridiculed the two investigators. He managed to sneak out the books right under their noses.

Q 15. The Invisible Man lost his temper and left the village of Iping in ruins. Comment.

अदृश्य आदमी ने अपना आपा खो दिया और आइपिंग गाँव को खंडहर बना दिया। टिप्पणी करें।

Ans. The Invisible Man aka Griffin had planned with Mr Marvel that they will get his books back. The plan went good until Mr Marvel was suspected of thievery and Mr Huxter started chasing him. His chase was brought to a halt by Griffin. However, the whole village also started chasing him.

Mr Marvel had Griffin's precious books. If he would have been caught, Griffin would have had a major setback. Hence, he started hurting the pursuers. Initially, he wanted to aid Mr Marvel's escape but then he lost his temper. He set to smite and overthrow people for the mere pleasure of causing harm.

Then he broke all the windows of the 'Coach and Horses' and thrust a street lamp through the parlour window of Mrs Gribble. The streets of Iping were left deserted, all kinds of stuff lay scattered and no soul was to be seen.

Q 16. Why did Mr Marvel want to resign from the post of Griffin's sidekick? Did Griffin let him go?

ग्रिफिन के सहायक पद से मि मार्वेल इस्तीफा क्यों देना चाहता था? क्या ग्रिफिन ने उसे जाने दिया?

Ans. Mr Marvel was able to get away with Griffin's things with some help from the latter. But he tried to sneak away from Griffin also. However, Griffin caught up with him and probably hurt him. He also threatened to kill Mr Marvel if he tried that sort of thing ever again.

Initially, Mr Marvel had to give in before Griffin as he was chosen for his work. He was also promised to be rewarded handsomely.

But perhaps, the heist that he had to do at Iping was too much to take for him. He no longer wanted to be a part of Griffin's plans. He told him that he was a very bad aid and would probably get his plans failed. But Griffin was not ready to let go of him. He could easily empower the short man and needed him to carry his things around. Moreover, Mr Marvel could prove to be of more help. He didn't want to lose this advantage by giving up his services.

Q 17. At Port Stowe, a mariner got talking to Mr Marvel. Describe their meeting in your own words. What kind of a person the mariner was?

पोर्ट स्टॉव पर एक नाविक ने मार्वेल के साथ बातचीत करनी शुरू की। उनकी बातचीत का अपने शब्दों में वर्णन करें। नाविक कैसा इंसान था?

Ans. Mr Marvel was sitting anxious on a bench in Port Stowe. A mariner came to him and got talking about a news published in the newspaper. It was about the Invisible Man. Mr Marvel was nervous. He tried to relate to the mariner that he knew many things about the Invisible Man. However, Griffin was just around him and started hurting him. He got up abruptly and leaving his listener hanging, left the place. The mariner was left irate. He shouted at Mr Marvel and said that he had no elementary manners.

The mariner appears to be a lonely sort of a guy who would seek company in awkward news and wouldn't mind talking to tramps. He is also easily influenced as he believes that the story of the Invisible Man was true because it came from a real place, equipped with names and details. He held his temper when Mr Marvel ignored him but when he lost it, he came out shouting curses at him.

Q 18. How did the people at the 'Jolly Cricketers' react when Mr Marvel came running to them asking for refuge?

'जॉली क्रिकेटर्स' पर खड़े लोगों ने मदद माँगने वाले मार्वेल की मदद कैसे की?

Ans. The atmosphere at the 'Jolly Cricketers' was relaxed when they heard shouting down the street. Suddenly, Mr Marvel opened the door and shouted that the Invisible Man was after him. He told the crowd that the Invisible Man wanted to murder him. The people there were quick to react and the policeman asked the door to be closed. The black bearded man said that Mr Marvel was safe. Then there was rapping on the door.

The barman provided Mr Marvel refuge. They were all brave and swift. They made a plan to catch the Invisible Man. The black bearded man got his revolver out, but the policeman told him that he just couldn't kill a man. He replied that he knew his laws and wanted to shoot at the legs.

Griffin entered through the back door and got Mr Marvel. But they all jumped to save him. Finally, struggle ended when the black bearded, man fired all ends out.

Q 19. "All men, however highly educated, retain some superstitious inklings." How did the eerie feelings take over Dr Kemp?

"हर आदमी, उच्च शिक्षत, कुछ न कुछ अंधविश्वास जरूर पालता है।" किस प्रकार एक ऐसी ही अवधारणा केंप के ऊपर आ गई थी?

Ans. Dr Kemp was busy in his study when the bell of his front door rang. He expected that someone would come up, but upon inquiring with his maid, he found that it was a runaway call. This made him very uneasy.

He worked till late and went to bed around two o'clock. But he got thirsty and came down. Near the stairs, he found a dark spot and wondered what it was. He was burdened with thoughts. He touched the stain and it was drying blood. When he came to his room, he found that the door-handle of his own room was blood-stained. His room was also in a mess and more blood was there. The bedclothes were depressed as if someone had been recently sitting there. Then he heard his own name being taken and heard a movement across the room. The 'eerie feelings' took over him at this point.

Q 20. Do you think that Griffin himself was responsible for his tragic end or the society forced him to turn against his own kind?

अपने दु:खद अन्त के लिए ग्रिफिन खुद जिम्मेदार था या समाज ने उसे खुद के खिलाफ कर दिया था? आप इसके बारे में क्या राय रखते हो?

Ans. Griffin was a very gifted scientist. But it is also true that he was eccentric. He is the only one to be blamed for his tragic end. He may derive sympathy from the reader when he was chased for being different. However, on a deeper level, we realise that he adopted many evil ways to get his wishes done.

When he ran out of money, he robbed his own father which led to his suicide. He also hurt the owner of the costume shop. Though he was misunderstood by the people at Great Portland street, where all the fiasco started, he burned the whole house down just to hide his discovery. He wanted to establish a reign of terror and believed that his invisibility provided him with godly powers. He turned against his own race and died tragically.

Q 21. Griffin got into the Omniums empty handed and left empty handed. How had his plan failed?

ग्रिफिन ऑमनियम्स के अंदर भी खाली हाथ गया था और वहाँ से खाली हाथ बाहर भी आया। उसकी योजना कैसे असफल हो गई?

Ans. Griffin was stark naked and without food and shelter in the streets of London. Then he got a brilliant idea. He managed to enter the huge shop.

He clambered up a collection of bedsteads and waited till the shop was completely empty. After the place was immersed in silence, Griffin got down. He went straight towards the clothing section and adorned many things- from socks to hat. Then his next hit was the food. Near the toy department, he had another brilliant idea. He could fake an appearance by using false items. Finally, he went to sleep and was at peace after a long time.

Unfortunately, he slept till late and the store opened. He was spotted. The workers ran after him. Griffin tried to hide but somebody saw him. He resorted to hurt his pursuers and created a mess at the store. Finally, he had to take all his clothes off to go out of sight.

Q 22. Griffin thought that as he was invisible, he could easily rob anyone. However, the hunchback made it a hard task. Elaborate.

ग्रिफिन ने सोचा कि अपनी अदृश्यता की वजह से वह आसानी से चोरी कर लेगा परंतु कुबड़े आदमी ने उसका काम कठिन कैसे कर दिया?

Ans. Griffin reached the shop of his desire in Drury Lane. There was no one in the shop and Griffin entered. The gate had a clanking bell and immediately the owner of the house, a short hunched man, came running down. Griffin tried to follow the man, but he sensed it and the quickness of his ear surprised Griffin a lot. The man was busy washing his plates when Griffin put some coal in the fire. Immediately, the man came running upstairs. When Griffin was following him on the stairs, he suddenly stopped and was just an inch away from Griffin's face.

Griffin was nearly caught when he was searching for clothes. This made the hunchback furious. He started locking the doors of the house and before Griffin could do anything, he was locked in a room. Griffin could hardly control himself and he knocked him out cold. He explained that the hunchback gave him no choice.

Q 23. How did Dr Kemp's plan to get the Invisible Man arrested fail?

ग्रिफिन को गिरफ्तार करने की केंप की योजना असफल कैसे हो गई?

Ans. Even before Dr Kemp had heard of the sinister works of the Invisible Man, he had decided to turn him over to the police. He had written a note the very night that Griffin came into his house, informing Colonel Adye about his presence.

Griffin was narrating the incidents that had led to his invisibility and further his encounter with Dr Kemp. Dr Kemp saw some men coming up to the house and he tried to keep Griffin busy. He asked about Griffin's plans. Just then, sounds were heard from downstairs. Dr Kemp knew that it was the police and he tried to divide Griffin's attention. But when Griffin tried to open the door, he blocked him. In an instant, Griffin realised that Dr Kemp had cheated him. He takes his clothes off, hits Dr Kemp as hard as he could and before anyone could make a move, he had escaped.

Q 24. How did Dr Kemp use the knowledge given to him by Griffin himself to get him arrested? Were his attempts fruitful?

ग्रिफिन द्वारा दी गई जानकारी को ग्रिफिन के खिलाफ केंप ने कैसे इस्तेमाल किया? क्या उसके प्रयास सही साबित हो पाए?

Ans. After the plan to get Griffin arrested failed, Dr Kemp informed Colonel Adye that Griffin was mad. He further said that Griffin must be stopped or he would next turn to kill people.

Dr Kemp used the knowledge given to him by Griffin against him. He wanted that every available man should be put to hunt. He wanted to stop Griffin from escaping.

He knew that the only thing that could stop him from leaving the place was his three books. Dr Kemp said that they must stop him from eating or sleeping and every single person should be on alert.

Dr Kemp further said that they should use dogs as they could smell him. Another important thing was that the food eaten by Griffin was visible until it had been absorbed. He also wanted powdered glass on the roads as Griffin was bare feet. Alas! Inspite of these elaborate plans, Griffin was able to sleep and eat.

Q 25. How did Griffin meet his tragic end?

ग्रिफिन का दु:खद अंत कैसे हुआ था?

Ans. Griffin was filled with murderous rage. His confidant, Dr Kemp, had cheated him. He decided to murder Dr Kemp to set an example.

He laid siege on his house. However, Dr Kemp was saved by two policemen and Griffin was hurt. Dr Kemp ran towards the village and Griffin followed. Dr Kemp kept running but he couldn't make up his mind about where to seek shelter. Meanwhile, many people saw him and hearing his shouts came out to help him. They started running towards him and tried to provide him with some cover.

As others were trying to defend Dr Kemp, Griffin started beating him. Dr Kemp held his broken arm and Griffin cried. Suddenly, a labourer hit him with a spade. Griffin started to bleed. They all held him down and he started crying for mercy. Dr Kemp asked everybody to leave him. However, it was too late and Griffin had died in the struggle. The 'gifted physicist' met a tragic end.

Q 26. Do you think that Dr Kemp was really a traitor as he cheated Griffin and let out all his secrets? Give reasons.

क्या आप डॉ. केंप को धोखेबाज मानते हो क्योंकि उसने ग्रिफिन को धोखा दिया और उसके सारे राज बता दिए? कारण दीजिए।

Ans. Griffin and Dr Kemp were old acquaintances and both were scientists. However, Griffin wanted to establish a reign of terror and Dr Kemp thought about the social conditions of the future.

Griffin was an eccentric scientist. He wanted to smite everyone who came in his way. On the other hand, Dr Kemp thought of the greater good. Even before Griffin had mentioned his sinister plans,

Dr Kemp had decided to turn him over to the police. After hearing his plans realising the threat that Griffin posed to the society, he was hell-bent upon capturing him.

Therefore, it is not right to call Dr Kemp a traitor. Though he had cheated Griffin, he was thinking about the betterment of the society. He wanted to save the society from the devil that was Griffin.

Q 27. What forced Griffin to burn down the house in Great Portland Street?

ग्रेट पोर्टलैंड स्ट्रीट वाले घर को ग्रिफिन ने आग के हवाले क्यों कर दिया था?

Ans. Griffin had found an accommodation in a slum near the Great Portland Street. He filled the room with the apparatus that he needed to carry on with his experiment.

His long labour bore fruit and he was able to make a woolen cloth disappear. Then he tried to make a cat invisible. The noises made by the cat brought her owner to Griffin's footsteps. She suspected him of vivisection. Next day, the landlord came asking questions. Griffin behaved rudely with him and threw him out.

This was a crisis situation. He carried out the experiment on himself and became invisible. However, he was insecure and thought that someone could understand what he was doing. He dismantled all his apparatus but still he was not sure. He feared that his discovery would become public. He burned down the house to cover his trails.

Q 28. What were the difficulties faced by Griffin to achieve his dream of invisibility? Were the ways adopted by him morally correct?

अदृश्य होने के अपने सपने पूरा करने के लिए ग्रिफिन ने कौन-कौन सी परेशानियाँ उठाई थी? क्या उसके द्वारा अपनाए गए तौर-तरीके नैतिक रूप से सही थे?

Ans. Light fascinated Griffin and he dropped medicine to pursue physics. He worked like a slave. After six months of hard labour, he found a general principle of pigments and refraction and deduced a formula.

He researched and concluded that to make something invisible in air; it must have the same refractive index as the air. He also knew that humans are also transparent theoretically. After six years of toil and with ideas in his mind, he went to London. He hid his experiments from everyone, even his professor.

For three more years, he fought with exasperation and realised that he was out of money. At this point, he robbed his father which led to his death. His secret nature made people suspicious. Finally at Great Portland Street, he had to carry out the experiment in haste. He burned the house down to cover his trails.

No, the methods that he adopted for achieving his dream were not moral. His ways were vile and sinister.

Q 29. Griffin was invisible. It was like having a godly power. Still, he cried with helplessness. Why did Griffin grow so much hopeless?

ग्रिफिन अदृश्य हो गया था। यह एक दैवीय शक्ति के समान था। फिर भी वह बेचारगी के साथ चिल्ला रहा था। ग्रिफिन इतना निराश कैसे हो गया?

Ans. Griffin was having a hard time adjusting with his newly acquired power. Even his walk was clumsy. He was filled with great joy though and his mind was busy in the things which he could do without being seen. Suddenly, he was hit from behind. The man, carrying the basket, was greatly surprised and this made Griffin laugh.

A cabman rushed to catch the basket and his hands met Griffin's neck. Griffin was hurt and the crowd rushed to the scene. Griffin was in the danger of being discovered. So, he ran away from the place. On the street, his feet got stamped, his shoulder got bruised and most of all, he was stark naked and thus caught a cold.

Griffin's initial happiness had flown away and he thought how he was going to get out of the mess he was in. He was feeling so helpless that he nearly cried.

Q 30. What had happened to Wicksteed? What effect did it have on the people of Burdock?

विकस्टीड को किस घटना का सामना करना पड़ा था? बॅर्डाक के लोगों पर इसका क्या असर हुआ था?

Ans. Mr Wicksteed was a man of forty-five or forty six. His demeanor could hardly entice anyone to cause any harm to him. But he was found brutally murdered.

The incidents, leading to his death, are not clear. The author says that his murder is a mystery as no one had seen what actually had happened. However, everyone suspected that it was the Invisible Man who carried out the killing.

The narration takes an imaginative turn. The author says that probably Griffin was filled with rage and carried an iron rod. The flying rod caught Mr Wicksteed's attention and he went after it. Griffin did not want to be discovered so he attacked him and as a result, Mr Wicksteed was killed. Burdock was immersed in a thrill of horror after this.

Questions based on Character Sketch

Q 1. What impression do you form about 'The Invisible Man'? Is he able to gain the reader's sympathy?

अदृश्य आदमी के बारे में आपकी क्या राय है? क्या उसे पाठकों की सहानुभूति मिल पाई?

Ans. The Invisible Man is given many names in the novel. At first, he is the stranger who arrives at Iping then he is the voice that startles everybody. However, his real name is Griffin.

Though he is the protagonist of the story, all his deeds are more like that of an antagonist. He is an eccentric scientist. He was very gifted but used his mind in a sinister way. He devised an experiment to become invisible and then started looting and murdering whoever came in his way. He is very irritable and impatient. He loses his temper over petty things and starts hurting others. He has lost all senses of conscience and doesn't feel sorry even after his burglary led to his father's death.

Although, he is lonely and seems to have been misunderstood from time to time, he fails to gain sympathy due to his murderous rage and evil ways.

Q 2. Mrs Hall was a strong woman. However, we see some flaws in her character. In the light of this statement, attempt her character sketch.

मिसेज हॉल एक निश्चयी महिला थी। फिर भी, उनमें भी कुछ चारित्रिक दोष थे। इस कथन के संदर्भ में उसका चरित्र-चित्रण कीजिए।

Ans. Janny Hall, better known as Mrs Hall, is the owner of the 'Coach and Horses' inn in Iping. The first time when we encounter her, she appears to be an opportunist. She gives the stranger a room in her inn without showing much concern to confirm his identity.

She is also a bit money-minded. She accommodates with Griffin's rudeness and awkward behaviour only because she was being paid. However, she has a courteous side also which we see when she tries to know about Griffin's physical impairment and shows sympathy towards his state.

She is superstitious and believes that her furniture was haunted. She is a dominating wife and doesn't shy away from giving her husband a lecture. Moreover, she can put her foot down if required. When she had enough of the stranger's rudeness, she decided to set him straight and stopped serving him. She replied in such an angry tone that Griffin had to back away.

Q 3. Mr Hall appears to be a meek man who is guided by his wife. What impression is he able to leave on you?

मि हॉल एक डरपोक और पत्नी संचालित आदमी थे। आपकी उनके बारे में क्या राय है?

Ans. George Hall or Mr Hall is the husband of Mrs Hall and drove the Iping conveyance. He is a drunkard and his wife manages the inn on her own. He believes in others quite easily and when Mr Teddy Henfrey told him about Griffin, he at once formed the perception that something unusual was up.

He has an investigative side also. He wanted to know the details about his guest and tried to inspect his room when he found it empty. However, he is only secondary to his wife and is very meek in front of her. He gets taken to task by her many times. George is also kind like his wife. When the dog attacked Griffin, he rushed to his room to see if he needed any kind of help.

Q 4. It was Mr Teddy Henfrey who started spreading the rumors about Griffin. What does this reveal about his character?

ग्रिफिन के बारे में अफवाह फैलाने वाला टेडी हेनफ्रे था। इस बात से उसके चरित्र के बारे में आप क्या समझ पाते हो?

Ans. Mr Teddy Henfrey is a clock repairman whom Mrs Hall uses in an attempt to find out more about Griffin. When he arrives, he is taken to Griffin's room and he is at once startled by his appearance.

He is quite inquisitive by nature and tries to find more about the stranger. He purposely tries to work slowly. But the silence in the room makes him nervous. He tries to talk but gets snubbed by Griffin. This irritated him a lot. He is also a gossipmonger. When he couldn't find anything more about the stranger, he started spreading rumors about him. He has a suspecting nature. He was the one who said that the stranger was perhaps wanted by the police and that is why kept himself covered.

Q 5. 'Curiosity killed that cat.' How far is this statement correct in the case of Mr Cuss?

'जिज्ञासा ने जासूसी का अंत कर दिया'। मि कस के संदर्भ में यह कथन किस हद तक सही है?

Ans. Mr Cuss, the general practitioner in the village of Iping, was a curious cat. The bandages of the Invisible Man excited his professional interest. He was also jealous of him when he got to know that he possessed so many bottles of different shapes and size filled with chemicals. He thinks that he is smart and devises a plan to arrange an interview with the stranger just to gain more information about him.

However, he is scared out of his wits when Griffin shows him his empty sleeve. At first, he behaves boldly but runs away when Griffin tweaks his nose by the invisible hand. Though scared, he reacts rationally after coming to his senses.

He thinks that he had probably gone mad or insane. Later, we see his investigative nature also. He tried to decipher Griffin's book with the help of Mr Bunting.

Q 6. Mr Bunting was one of the educated members of the Iping village. What impression is he able to leave on the reader?

आइपिंग के शिक्षित लोगों में से मि बंटिंग भी एक थे। पाठकों पर उनका क्या प्रभाव है?

Ans. Mr Bunting is the vicar of the Iping village and thus is held in very high esteem by his fellow villagers. He is a rational being and when Mr Cuss narrates to him the story of his interview with the Invisible Man, he tries to calm him and get his facts right. He was suspicious about the things that Mr Cuss narrated and considered it to be a 'most remarkable story'.

We see that he is also very bold and brave. When the Invisible Man was robbing them, he didn't get scared. He kept himself cool. He didn't act in panic and tried to see who the robber was. Later, we see his investigative nature also. He tried to decipher Griffin's book with the help of Mr Cuss. However, he was quite showy and tried to hide the fact that he had forgotten all his Greek.

Q 7. Attempt the character sketch of Mr Jaffers.

मि जैफर्स का चरित्र-चित्रण कीजिए।

Ans. Mr Bobby Jaffers is the constable of the Iping village who comes with a warrant to arrest the Invisible Man. He appears to be a resolute man and takes his work rather seriously. He comments that head or no head, he got to arrest the man and that is what he will do.

He is also a very brave man. When the invisible head confronted him, he rapped his point that he was there to arrest him and didn't shiver. He is strong but was no match for his invisible enemy and gets beaten up. Though, he couldn't see the stranger, he thought that it was some kind of trick.

He is quick to react and at once realised that the Invisible Man was trying to escape. Obviously, he is not able to hold the unseen and the Invisible Man gets away from his custody. Apparently, he was hurt for he had failed to complete his duties and later we find him sunk in gloom.

Q 8. Mr Marvel was supposed to be an ally of Griffin. However, he was an opportunist and was very much responsible for his ill-fate. In the light of this statement, attempt his character sketch.

मार्वेल को ग्रिफिन का साथी माना जाता था। लेकिन मार्वेल एक अवसरवादी था और ग्रिफिन के दुर्भाग्य के लिए जिम्मेदार भी था। इस कथन के संदर्भ में उसका चरित्र-चित्रण कीजिए।

Ans. Mr Thomas Marvel is a short, fat man. He gives the impression of a tramp- the shabby hat, the charity boots, his clothes and his homeless lifestyle. The narrator says that he does everything in a leisurely manner which means that he is a lazy guy. Griffin makes him his sidekick even though he himself considers him stupid and good for nothing. He is a coward little man and is unable to stand up to Griffin. He becomes his partner in crime but cheats him.

He is also a very opportunistic guy. The first chance that he gets, he tries to sneak away from Griffin, but fails. The second time, he manages to run away with all his money and his three books. He is very clever in the sense that he himself gets arrested as he knew Griffin was after him. Moreover, he kept the three books for himself in the hope of solving their mystery- an act of foolishness.

Q 9. What impression do you form about the owner of the costume shop (the hunchback), the shop that Griffin looted in Drury Lane?

साज-सज्जा की दुकान के कुबड़े मालिक जिसे ग्रिफिन ने ड्रूरी लेन में लूटा था, के बारे में आपकी क्या राय है?

Ans. We encounter the hunchback- a name given to him by Griffin and Dr Kemp- when Griffin narrates the incidents that happened in Drury Lane. We don't know his name but he owned a shabby costume shop. He is a short, slight, hunched and a beetle-browed man with long arms and very short bandy legs.

Griffin sneaks into his shop only to realise that the man has a very sharp hearing sense. He nearly catches Griffin moving here and there in his house. He has no table manners and is irritable. He is also very cunning. He tries to see who was in his house by sneaking slowly upstairs. He also tried to lock each and every room of his house so that he could catch the culprit. He was so clever that Griffin had to knock him down to steal what he wanted.

Q 10. Dr Kemp was a confidant of Griffin but upon realising that he was insane, he thought of the greater good and tried to turn him over. In the light of this statement, attempt his character sketch.

डॉ. केंप ग्रिफिन के राजदार थे, लेकिन यह जानने पर कि ग्रिफिन पागल हो चुका है, उसने सामाजिक हित की बात सोची और उसे धोखा दिया। इस कथन के संदर्भ में उसका चरित्र-चित्रण करें।

Ans. Like Griffin, Dr Kemp was also a scientist who lived in Burdock. Actually, they both had gone to the same college. He was a tall and slender young man with flaxen hair and a moustache almost white.

He is ambitious which is clear from the fact that he wanted recognition for his achievements.

But then, he is also a speculative philosopher. The night that Griffin comes to his house, Dr Kemp is working on a remote speculation of social conditions of the future.

He is a very calm and sensible man. He doesn't get scared by the invisible intruder. He kept himself cool when the murder threat arrived. He lays his own life on the line to get Griffin arrested which shows that he was also very brave.

However, his sense of judgement sometimes gets awry. He sent the maid alone to deliver the note and also ran away leaving the two policemen behind.

Q 11. Colonel Adye was a man of duty but met an unfortunate end. What impression is he able to leave on the readers?

कर्नल एडी एक कर्त्तव्यनिष्ठ इंसान था। अफसोस उसकी मौत दुःखद तरीके से हुई। पाठकों पर इसकी क्या प्रतिक्रिया हुई?

Ans. Colonel Adye is the Chief of Police in Burdock. Our first impression of him is that of a brave man. He comes running to arrest the Invisible Man residing in Dr Kemp's house.

Then we see him as a person who takes decisions very swiftly. However, he blindly followed what Dr Kemp asked him to do and didn't give his own opinion which shows that instead of being a leader, he was more of a follower.

He is a moral being and opposes the idea of spreading powdered glass on the roads at it was 'unsportsmanlike'. But, Dr Kemp pursued and he obliged. We again see a glimpse of his bravery and foolishness also when he tries to fight the Invisible Man having a gun. This results in his getting shot.

Q 12. Mr Heelas ditched Dr Kemp in his time of need. In the light of this statement, comment on his character.

जरूरत पड़ने पर मि हीलास ने डॉ. केंप को धोखा दे दिया था। इस कथन के संदर्भ में उसके चरित्र पर एक टिप्पणी लिखिए।

Ans. Mr Heelas was the next door neighbour to Dr Kemp. He was one of the sturdy minority who refused to believe in the story of the Invisible Man and regarded it as nonsense though his wife did. When it was proclaimed that everyone should be on high alert, he insisted upon walking about his garden as if nothing had happened. This shows his casual view towards the rumors and his 'seeing then believing' attitude.

However, he comes about as a coward who would not open his door to help his neighbour in distress. Griffin was after Dr Kemp. When Mr Heelas woke up and saw his neighbour's house, he at once realised that the Invisible Man was after him. Dr Kemp came running to him, but he denied his entry. Perhaps, he was trying to save his family, but this was not a moral act.

Character Sketches

The Invisible Man

The Invisible Man is given many names in the novel. Though he is the protagonist of the story, all his deeds are more like that of an antagonist. He is an eccentric scientist. He loses his temper over petty things and starts hurting others. He has lost all sense of conscience.

Mrs Hall

Mrs Hall, is the owner of the Coach and Horses inn in Iping. She appears to be an opportunist. She gives the stranger a room in her inn. She accommodates with Griffins rudeness and awkward behaviour only because she was being paid. She is a dominating wife and doesn't shy away from giving her husband a lecture. When she had enough of the stranger's rudeness, she decided to set him straight and stopped serving him.

Mr Hall

Mr Hall is the husband of Mrs Hall and drove the Iping conveyance. He is a drunkard and his wife manages the inn on her own. He believes when Teddy Henfrey told him about Griffin. He wanted to know the details about his guest and tried to inspect his room when he found it empty. However, He gets taken to task by her many times. George is also kind like his wife. When the dog attacked Griffin, he rushed to his room to see if he needed any kind of help.

Mr Teddy Henfrey

Teddy Henfrey is a clock repairman is taken to Griffin's room. He tries to find more about the stranger. He tries to talk but gets snubbed by Griffin. This irritated him a lot. He is also a gossipmonger. When he couldn't find anything more about the stranger, he started spreading rumors about him.

चरित्र चित्रण

अदृश्य आदमी

अदृश्य आदमी को उपन्यास में कई नाम दिए गए हैं। हालाँकि वह कहानी का मुख्य पात्र है पर उसका काम नकारात्मक रहा है। वह एक सनकी वैज्ञानिक है। छोटी-छोटी बातों पर वह अपना आपा खो देता है और दूसरों को चोट पहुँचाना शुरू कर देता है। वह अपने आप में नहीं होता और नैतिक पतन की ओर चला जाता है।

मिसेज हॉल

मिसेज हॉल आइपिंग के धर्मशाला कोच एंड हॉर्सेज की मालकिन हैं। वह एक अवसरवादी महिला है। ग्रिफिन को उसने अपने धर्मशाला में एक कमरा दिया था। ग्रिफिन के बुरे व्यवहार और बदतमीजियों को भी वह सिर्फ इसलिए झेल जाती है क्योंकि उसे उसके बदले में पैसे मिल रहे होते हैं। वह अपने पति को भी ताने मारने से बाज नहीं आती है और हमेशा उसकी खिंचाई करती रहती है। अदृश्य आदमी के व्यवहार से जब वह दु:खी हो गई तो उसने उसे खाना देना बंद कर दिया था।

मि हॉल

मि हॉल मिसेज हॉल के पति हैं और धर्मशाला परविहन का ध्यान रखते हैं। वह शराबी है और मिसेज हॉल धर्मशाला को खुद सँभाल रही होती है। टेडी हेनफ्रे के कहने पर उसने ग्रिफिन की विचित्रता का अनुमान पूरे भरोसे के साथ कर लिया था। मि हॉल अजनबी के बारे में जानना चाहता था और जब उसने उसका कमरा खाली देखा तो उसकी जाँच भी की थी। मि हॉल को कई बार अपनी पत्नी के गुस्से का सामना भी करना पड़ा था। मि हॉल दयालु स्वभाव का भी था। जब एक कुत्ते ने ग्रिफिन पर हमला कर दिया था तो वह ग्रिफिन के कमरे में उसे मदद के लिए पूछने गया था।

मि टेडी हेनफ्रे

टेडी घड़ी मरम्मत करने का काम करता था। जब वह ग्रिफिन के कमरे में घड़ी ठीक करने गया था तब उसने उसके बारे में और भी ज्यादा जानकारी लेने की कोशिश की थी। उसने ग्रिफिन से बात करने की कोशिश की पर उसे डाँट दिया गया था जिससे वह नाराज भी हो गया था। टेडी अफवाह फैलाने में भी माहिर था। जब उसे ग्रिफिन के बारे में कुछ पता नहीं चला तो उसने उसके बारे में अफवाह फैलाना शुरू कर दिया था।

Mr Cuss

Mr Cuss, the general practitioner in the village of Iping, was a curious cat. He was also jealous of him when he got to know that he possessed so many bottles of different shapes and size filled with chemicals. He devised a plan to arrange an interview with the stranger just to gain more information about him. However, he is scared out of his wits when Griffin shows him his empty sleeve.

मि कस

मि कस आइपिंग गाँव में डॉक्टर थे और बड़े जिज्ञासु थे। ग्रिफिन से उसे ईर्ष्या थी और वह उसके रसायनों से भरी बोतलों को देख कर परेशान हो जाता था। उसने एक योजना बनाई ताकि वह उससे मिल सके व उसके बारे में और जानकारी हासिल कर सके। जब उसे ग्रिफिन ने अपना अदृश्य हाथ दिखाया तो उसकी बुद्धि खराब हो गई थी और वह डर कर वहाँ से भाग गया था।

Mr Bunting

Mr Bunting is the vicar of the Iping village and thus is held in very high esteem by his fellow villagers. His house was the first to be hit by the evil deeds of the Invisible Man. Later, he was also humiliated by him.

मि बंटिंग

मि बंटिंग गाँव के चर्च में पादरी थे और इस वजह से पूरे गाँव में सम्मानीय थे। ग्रिफिन के करतूतों का पहला शिकार मि बंटिंग का ही घर बना था। बाद में ग्रिफिन ने मि बंटिंग की बेइज्जती भी कर दी थी।

Mr Jaffers

Mr Jaffers is the constable of the Iping village who comes with a warrant to arrest the Invisible Man. He takes his work rather seriously. He comments that head or no head, he got to arrest him and that is what he will do. Apparently, he was hurt for he had failed to complete his duties and later we find him sunk in gloom.

मि जैफर्स

मि जैफर्स आइपिंग गाँव में सिपाही था और गिरफ्तारी के वारंट के साथ वह ग्रिफिन को पकड़ने आए थे। वे कर्त्तव्यनिष्ठ थे। उसने कहा था सिर हो या न हो वह उसे गिरफ्तार करके रहेंगे। अफसोस कि वे ग्रिफिन को गिरफ्तार नहीं कर पाए और अपनी कर्त्तव्यनिष्ठता साबित नहीं कर पाए। इससे उन्हें घोर निराशा हुई थी।

www.ingramcontent.com/pod-product-compliance
Ingram Content Group UK Ltd.
Pitfield, Milton Keynes, MK11 3LW, UK
UKHW021700190726
13853UKWH00001B/376

9 789351 765301